DIALOGUE WITH

WITH

JEAN
PIAGET

DIALOGUES IN CONTEMPORARY PSYCHOLOGY SERIES

Richard I. Evans, Series Editor

DIALOGUE WITH

JEAN PIAGET

Richard I. Evans

Translated by
Eleanor Duckworth

PRAEGER

PRAEGER SPECIAL STUDIES • PRAEGER SCIENTIFIC

Library of Congress Cataloging in Publication Data

Evans, Richard Isadore, 1922-
  Dialogue with Jean Piaget.

    (Dialogues in contemporary psychology series)
    Reprint. Originally published: Jean Piaget, the man
and his ideas. New York : Dutton 1973. With a new
introd.
    Bibliography: p.
    Includes index.
    1. Piaget, Jean, 1896-   . 2. Psychologists—
Switzerland—Biography. 3. Cognition in children.
4. Psychology. I. Piaget, Jean, 1896-   . II. Title.
III. Series: Evans, Richard Isadore, 1922-   . Dialogues
with notable contributors to personality theory.
BF109.P5E93 1981   155.4′13′0924   81-15374
ISBN 0-03-059931-8   AACR2

Pages xxii—xli reprinted by permission of the American Heri-
tage Publishing Company from *Horizons*, Winter 1971. Pages
xlii—lxi reprinted by permission of *The Columbia Forum*, Columbia University, from *The Columbia Forum*, Fall 1969, and
the author. Pages 105—179 reprinted by permission of Clark
University Press from E. G. Boring et. al (EDs.), *A History of
Psychology in Autobiography*, Vol. IV.

Published in 1981 by Praeger Publishers
CBS Educational and Professional Publishing
a Division of CBS Inc.
521 Fifth Avenue, New York, New York 10175 U.S.A.

© 1973 by Richard I. Evans and
    1981 by Praeger Publishers

123456789 145 987654321
Printed in the United States of America

To
my lovely wife
and children

Introduction to the Praeger Edition

With Jean Piaget's death on September 17, 1980, the contents of this volume take on a new historical dimension. This volume contains perhaps Dr. Piaget's final overview of his extensive contributions. In his public lectures and published works following the original publication of this volume, Dr. Piaget continued to elaborate on many of the points he made in the context of our dialogue. I am pleased that this volume contains Dr. Piaget's autobiography and David Elkind's marvelous introduction. I hope that my summary of his theories and their interface with those of Erikson, Skinner, and Freud will contribute to the historical perspective on Piaget's substantial contributions.

I am delighted that the appearance of the Praeger edition will make available to a new audience this document that reflects such a lucid statement of so profound a contributor to the understanding of the development of our mental processes.

ACKNOWLEDGMENTS

In the long process involved in filming and taping the dialogues with Jean Piaget and transcribing, editing, and integrating them into the present volume, I am indebted to a great many individuals. Though space prohibits mentioning everyone who so kindly assisted in this venture, I wish to express my appreciation to at least some of these individuals.

As I prepared the structure of the dialogue, valuable suggestions came from Dr. Hans Furth of Catholic University. His contribution is very much appreciated, as is the assistance given by psychology student Mrs. Alice Bane during the early stages of preparation of the manuscript.

Grateful acknowledgment is also made to the University of Houston for permission to utilize the printed texts of the filmed and taped dialogue. Mr. James Bauer of the University of Houston, who functioned in the demanding role of technical director for the taping and filming sessions, should be mentioned among those who have greatly assisted me.

I wish to express my thanks to Mrs. Bette Keating, who with great patience and care handled the demanding chore of collating, rechecking, and typing the final form of the manuscript.

I am grateful for support from the National Science Foundation, without which this project could not have been implemented.

Thanks are accorded to Dr. David Elkind of the University of Rochester for allowing us to use as part of the present volume his fine introduction to Piaget's ideas, which appeared first in *Horizon* magazine. (Our thanks also to *Horizon* magazine for permission to reproduce the article.) We also appreciate Dr. Piaget's willingness to allow us to reprint his autobiography, which first appeared in Boring *et al., History of Psychology Through Autobiography* and his article "Genetic Epistemology," which first appeared in the *Columbia Forum* (our thanks to Clark University Press and *Columbia Forum* for permission to reproduce these materials).

Ms. Eleanor Duckworth, in her own right an acknowledged authority on Piaget's work, did a superb job in translating Piaget's French responses into English. Her overall interest in this project, films as well as this book, is greatly appreciated. Dr. Guy Cellerier, of the Jean Jacques Rousseau Institute, performed the important role of completing the on-the-scene translations in the discussion between Dr.

Piaget and myself, and his fine handling of this role is gratefully acknowledged.

Thanks are accorded psychology graduate student Harvey Ginsburg who made valuable contributions both editorially and in checking out relevant bibliographical sources. Of course, his collaboration along with that of Dr. William J. Krossner, Jr. (whose work at the Harvard University Center for Cognitive Studies provided a fine background for this task) on the overview of Piaget's ideas that is Part VII of this volume is particularly appreciated. The support and interest of Psychology Department colleague Dr. Gerald Gratch, a significant researcher of Piaget's concepts, is very much appreciated as well. For example, he was responsible for the inclusion of Piaget's autobiography, which appears as Part VIII of this volume.

Finally, the wonderful cooperation of Professors Jean Piaget and Barbel Inhelder, who along with Dr. Piaget appears in the filmed portion of the dialogue, cannot be emphasized enough. Not only were they willing to participate in the filming and audio-taping sessions that were involved in this project, but their genuine kindness and good humor during the course of what was surely an unfamiliar role for them will long be remembered by us all.

RICHARD I. EVANS
Professor of Psychology
University of Houston

CONTENTS

INTRODUCTION

PART A: *Some Observations on the Dialogue Style and Overview of Other Parts of the Book*

To avoid possible misunderstandings about the goals of the dialogue style utilized in much of this volume, some background perspective may be of value.

The present book constitutes the seventh in a series based on dialogues with some of the world's outstanding contributors to the understanding of personality. Designed as a hopefully innovative teaching device, the series was launched in 1957 with completion of dialogues with the late Carl Jung and Ernest Jones supported by a grant from the Fund for the Advancement of Education, and is being continued under a current grant from the National Science Foundation. A basic purpose of the project is to produce for teaching purposes a series of films which introduce the viewer to our distinguished interviewees' major contributions to the field of personality psychology and human behavior. These films may also serve as documents of increasing value in the history of the behavioral sciences.*

The books in this series are based on edited transcripts of the dialogue, including the text of audiotaped discussions apart from those used in the films. These dialogues not only serve to introduce the reader to the contributor's major ideas and points of view, but also convey through the extemporaneousness of the dialogue style a feeling for the personality of the contributor.

When we completed the first book in the series based on dialogues with Jung and Jones (Evans, 1964) we thought the word "conversation" could best be used in the title to describe its process and content. However, we soon discovered that this seemed to imply to some potential readers of the book something a bit more casual and superficial than we had intended. Even though an attempt is made to emphasize spontaneity in our dialogues with our participants, we do not wish it to detract from any significance that the content may have. We would hope that a relatively informal discussion with an outstanding contributor to a discipline, as he seriously examines his own work, will not be of less significance by virtue of its informality than more formal presentations of his work.

A more detailed description of the philosophy and techniques of this project is reported elsewhere (Evans, 1969c). However, a few points bearing on

* The films are distributed by CCM Films, 34 MacQuesten Parkway, S., Mt. Vernon, New York 10550.

the content of these volumes might be emphasized here. First of all, since the questions are intended to reflect many of the published writings of the interviewee, it might be expected that a comprehensive summary of his work is evoked. However, because of the selectivity necessary in developing the questions so that the discussion can be completed within a limited time interval, it would not be fair to say the results of these sessions—either in the films, which reflect the content emanating from only about half the time spent with the participant, or even in the books, which reflect about twice the amount of time—necessarily provide the basis for an inclusive summary of the contributor's work.

In more general terms, we are presenting a teaching technique that could become an additional means of compensating for a trend observed among many of our students today—an increasing reliance on secondary sources to gain information concerning our major contributors in the various disciplines. The material resulting from our dialogues provides a novel "original source" exposure to the ideas of leading contributors to a discipline. Hopefully, this in turn may stimulate the reader to go back to the original writings of the interviewee, where his ideas are developed more fully than could possibly be done through our "dialogue." In fact, the term "dialogue" was finally adopted instead of "conversation" to describe our content and method. It implies a more programmed content than the term conversation. However, the interpretation of the term "dialogue" sometimes also implies a "challenge" or a confrontation with the individual being "interviewed." Furthermore, to some the term "dialogue" suggests that the questioner is simply using the individual being questioned as a tool to project his own (the questioner's) teaching role into the situation.

My own goals here would preclude either of these interpretations of the term "dialogue." It is my intention that these "dialogues" reflect a constructive, novel method of teaching, and I see my interviewer role neither as the center of focus, nor as "critical challenger." I would feel that the purpose of this project has been realized if I am perceived as having merely provided a medium through which our distinguished interviewees can express their views. It might be mentioned here that the willingness of our interviewees to so generously contribute their time to these efforts is a direct reflection of their interest in the teaching aims of this project. This became evident from the very beginning, for example, in a letter from the late Carl Jung, reproduced in the first chapter of *Conversations with Carl Jung and Reactions from Ernest Jones* (Evans, 1964). Furthermore, using such sessions primarily as a background for critical examination of the views of the participants might better be left to another type of project, since even if this "critical set" were to be emphasized in my questioning, it might be difficult both to introduce the reader to the contributor's views and to criticize them as well, within the limited time commitment. In fact, I would expect that some of the individuals who agreed to participate in our project would not have done so if they had sensed that this would become primarily the context for a critical attack on their work.

As was the case with subjects of the earlier books in the series (Jung and Jones [Evans, 1964], Fromm [Evans, 1966], Erikson [Evans, 1969a], Skinner [Evans, 1968], Arthur Miller [Evans, 1969b], Gordon Allport[1] [Evans, 1970]), it is hoped that the dialogue presentation allows the reader to be introduced to or to reexamine some of Piaget's ideas through a relatively informal approach, as they develop from the particular points of view inherent in the questions which guide the discussion. It should be pointed out, however, that in his writings, as Piaget expresses himself in his own unique style, he has the opportunity to rewrite and to polish until he deems the finished product satisfactory. In the spontaneity of our discussion, however, he is called upon to develop his ideas extemporaneously and he is hampered further in the translation from French to English. But I hope that this element of spontaneity assists in penetrating to the "man behind the book" while losing none of the ideas central to Piaget's thought. Because preservation of this natural- ness of communication is essential to the purposes of each volume in this series, few liberties have been taken with the basic content of Piaget's responses to my questions, as translated by Eleanor Duckworth, although some editorial license had to be exercised to shift effectively from oral to printed communication in the service of accuracy, readability, clarity, and gram- matical construction.

The dialogue as it is presented here duplicates in-

[1] We were very pleased when the last book in this series, *Gordon Allport: The Man and His Ideas*, was honored by re- ceiving the 1971 American Psychological Foundation Media Award in the Book category.

sofar as possible the tenor of the exchange between Dr. Piaget and myself as it actually took place. In spite of some of the editing which was necessary in both Piaget's responses, as indicated above, and my questions, it was a pleasant surprise to review our hours of discussion content and see how few deletions and alterations were required. We hope this makes available to the reader some reactions not readily obtainable from Piaget's traditional didactic presentations or from some of the secondary sources on Piaget's work in the literature.

In order to expand the reader's knowledge of Piaget and his ideas, I have added some additional sections to this book. In the introductory section I have included a lucid introduction to Piaget by the highly regarded authority on Piaget, David Elkind, entitled: "Measuring Young Minds." Also in the introductory section is a significant paper by Piaget himself entitled "Genetic Epistemology," which was presented at a conference held a few years ago at Columbia University. In it he clearly shows the parallel between his search for the roots of knowledge in the history of man and his ingenious work examining the development of thought processes in the child.

At the end of the book I have included an overview of Piaget's model of intellectual development which I wrote in conjunction with Dr. William J. Krossner and University of Houston psychology doctoral candidate Harvey Ginsburg. The purpose of this part is to "flesh out" and provide more detail on some sections of the dialogue and define some of the key concepts which Piaget uses. Also, since Piaget and I, at least briefly, refer to Freud, Skinner, and Erikson, I thought the reader might find our views on the similarities between Piaget and these other notable psychologists of some interest.

Finally, I have concluded this volume with Piaget's fascinating autobiography, updating a few paragraphs and adding a listing of his various publications.

Part B: *Measuring Young Minds:*
An Introduction to the Ideas
of Jean Piaget
by David Elkind

He is still, at seventy-four, a familiar sight in the streets of Geneva, pedaling by on his bicycle or trudging along—tall, stoop-shouldered, and somewhat portly—as he mulls over some new problem arising out of his most recent investigations into the mystery of how knowledge develops in the young human being. A pipe juts from between his teeth, and a mass of fine white hair billows out around his blue beret. Indoors and close up, the beret is gone, but the pipe remains, the meerschaum lining of its bowl burned a deep amber; as he puffs on it, a forefinger locked around the stem, the eyes behind the horn-rimmed glasses narrow with interest when a question is being put to him. He answers—in French— in clear and unambiguous language, perhaps interjecting a mild joke; and although his manner is one of Old World charm (unless he feels his precious time is being imposed on to no good purpose, when he can turn direct and abrupt), he also seems to emanate an aura of intellectual presence not unlike the aura of dramatic presence emanated by a great actor.

Does this sound like the description of a revolutionary? Hardly: the famous Swiss psychologist Jean Piaget appears, in person, more like a benign if startlingly percipient paterfamilias; and indeed, he is the father of three grown children. (More significantly, he possesses a remarkable degree of empathy for children and ability to communicate with them—qualities that have helped him very considerably in his work.) Yet the findings he has gleaned, and the theory he has constructed after more than forty years of studying the development of intelligence, are effecting a veritable Copernican revolution in our understanding of the growth and functioning of the human mind.

Jean Piaget showed his scientific promise early: at ten, he observed a rare part-albino sparrow and wrote a note about it, which he submitted to a scientific journal. The journal published the note—the first of the vast number of articles and more than thirty books Piaget has authored and seen into print. Soon after, he became an apprentice of the curator of the museum in his native town of Neuchâtel. The curator, a biologist, had a fine collection of mollusks, Piaget began to observe mollusks on his own and again published his findings in Swiss scientific journals. By the time he was sixteen he had quite a respectable bibliography; indeed, so respectable that he was offered, sight unseen, the post of curator of the mollusk collection at the museum in Geneva—an offer he had to turn down because he was still in high school.

Although biology was Piaget's first love, and the discipline in which he received his doctorate with a thesis on mollusks, he did not find it entirely satisfying. For one thing, he was interested in philosophical questions regarding the problem of "how we know," and his work in biology was not a sufficiently direct route to solving that problem. Then, too, he realized that he lacked the dexterity—and perhaps the stomach —for such activities as dissection.

After receiving his doctorate, Piaget tried out a number of occupations that he hoped might prove better suited to his talents and interests. He flirted with psychoanalysis and spent six months at the Burghölzli Psychiatric Clinic in Zurich (where Jung once worked). While Piaget was intrigued by Freudian theory (he presented a paper on dreams at a conference that Freud attended), clinical practice had little appeal for him. After this he went to Paris, where he worked at the school in which Alfred Binet had originated the intelligence test. It was while testing children in Binet's laboratory school that Piaget discovered—or invented—his own scientific discipline.

Piaget found that in administering mental tests to children he could not only combine his biological and philosophical interests but could perform experiments that required little in the way of dexterity. The child is, first of all, a growing organism to whom all the principles of biological development apply. He is a thinking organism, who comes to know, in one way or another, about the social and physical reality within which he functions. By testing the child's understanding of the physical, biological, and social worlds at successive age levels, Piaget hoped to find an answer to the question of how we acquire knowledge. In effect Piaget had created an experimental philosophy that sought to answer philosophical questions by putting them to empirical test. He called this new discipline "genetic epistemology."

To put Piaget's enterprise in perspective we must know something about the scientific *Zeitgeist*, or spirit of the times. In the twenties and early thirties social science in America and England had become rigidly environmentalist: in contrast to the theories of hereditary taint that still predominated in European discussions of mental retardation and criminal behavior, the environmentalists stressed the brutal conditions under which criminals and familial retardates were reared.

In America the emphasis on environmental factors was reflected in an almost total preoccupation with learning, which psychologists defined as the modification of behavior due to experience. Psychology textbooks spent pages laying to rest the ghost of so-called instincts, the innate behavior patterns. While animals had instincts, the student was taught, man for the most part did not: even maturation, conceived as the unfolding of genetically determined (in part, at least) behavior patterns, was regarded as unscientific. Not surprisingly, maturationists such as Arnold Gesell, whose careful observations were a model of good descriptive psychology, fell into scientific disrepute.

In sharp contrast to the environmentalism of American social science was the nativism of European psychology. This nativism, a belief in the hereditary determination of personal and social traits, was later subverted into the racist doctrines of Nazism. From Europe had come Gestalt psychology, which suggested that experience never came to us "in the raw" but always in an organized fashion; that, for example, notes played in sequence are heard as a melody and not just as a sequence of notes. Such organizations were, according to Gestalt psychologists, determined by innate organizers or mental structures. When many Gestalt psychologists immigrated to America to escape Hitler, they ran head on into environmentalism. And the winds of the nature-nurture controversy blew hot and strong.

Piaget declined to take sides; he saw himself as "the man in the middle," the man who viewed nature and nurture as always relative to each other. His early experiments with mollusks had suggested that the influences of environment and heredity were reciprocal, with neither absolute, and his first observations of children convinced him that this relativism of nature and nurture extended to the development of human intelligence as well. He discovered that children harbored notions concerning nature and the physical world that they had neither inherited nor learned in the classic sense. He found, for example, that young children believed the moon followed them when they went for a walk at night, that dreams came in through the window while they were asleep, and that anything that moved, including waves and windblown curtains, was alive.

Where did such ideas come from? They were not inborn; because something that is inborn does not change and most children give up these ideas as they grow older. Likewise, the ideas could not have been learned from adults, because adults do not think in this way and would hardly teach such things to children. And since children everywhere, from completely different backgrounds, harbor such ideas, the ideas could not have been learned.

Piaget's answer to this puzzle was that the child's ideas about the world were "constructions" that involved both mental structures and experience. Like the Gestalt psychologists, Piaget argued that experience does not come to us raw but is organized by our intelligence. His advance over Gestalt psychology was his argument that the organizing structures are not fixed at birth but develop in a regular sequence of stages related to age. While the changes with age imply the role of experience, their orderliness reflects an interaction between nature and nurture. Piaget set out to discover the principles that govern this interaction.

One of the developmental principles revealed by Piaget's work is that mental growth occurs by integration and substitution and not solely by the addition of new facts. The child of three or four already has an elementary concept of quantity: confronted with two identical glasses of orangeade filled to the same level, he would say that both had the "same to drink." But if the orangeade from one glass were poured into a tall, narrow beaker while he looked on, the child would say, Piaget found, that the tall glass had "more to drink" than the shorter one. Not until about six or seven do most children understand that changing the shape of a quantity does not change its amount. The young child has a concept of quantity, but it is clearly a different concept from the one held by older children and adults: he thinks the amount of liquid can be gauged by its level without taking its width into account. Older children and adults, however, assess liquid quantities by taking both height and width into consideration.

This is mental growth by integration, wherein a new, higher-level idea (amount is determined by height and width) is formed by the integration of two lower-level ideas (amount is determined by height *or* width). It suggests that mental growth is an expanding upward spiral in which the same problems are attacked at successive age levels but are resolved more completely and more successfully at each higher level. Something similar occurs in science generally. The ancient Greeks talked about "atoms," but their concept of atoms was quite different from that held by modern physicists; even so, some of their ideas about atoms coincide, or are integrated, with our own. Growth by integration means the progression from a primitive to a more mature, differentiated, and elaborate concept.

The principle growth by integration is particularly important in its application to education. By and large, our educational system is concerned with growth by the accretion of facts. Now, certain facts—the capital of Greece, the number of days in a week, and the meaning of the abbreviation C.O.D.—are either right or wrong: the capital of Greece is Athens, and no other answer is correct. But a child who thinks that quantity is gauged by one dimension alone does not have a "wrong" idea; he simply has a *different* one from ours. Piaget's work indicates that we must expand our view of knowledge to include not only facts that are correct but also concepts that may be the same as or different from ours without being either right or wrong.

Mental growth also occurs by substitution. In areas such as moral judgment and ideas about nature, the primitive ideas held by young children are simply replaced by more mature ideas as the children grow older. Piaget found, for example, that young children judge a person according to the amount of damage he does rather than on the basis of his intentions. He told children two stories: in the first a child helping his mother to set the table trips and breaks twelve cups, and in the second a child who has been forbidden to climb up to a cupboard for jam does so and breaks one cup. Young children feel that the first child needs punishing the most since he broke twelve cups, while older children tend to find the second child more worthy of punishment because he intentionally disobeyed his mother.

Piaget obtained similar results when he queried children about lying. Again, children of different age groups were presented with two stories. In one story a boy told his mother he had seen a pink elephant dancing in the street to the tune of an organ played by a monkey. In the other a boy reported that he had received a grade of one hundred on an arithmetic test when in fact he had received only a sixty-five. Young children said the child who told the elephant story was more to be blamed because his lie was "bigger." Older children said that the boy who told the story about the elephant had meant to amuse his mother and was therefore less culpable than the one who said he had received a perfect grade in order consciously to deceive his mother.

In these studies and in many others like them, Piaget found that young children have an "objective morality," based on the amount of damage done, whereas older children have a "subjective morality," based on the subject's intentions. This developmental progression from objective to subjective morality is, however, only relative, and we adults often slip into an objective morality—particularly when we are dealing with children. A child, for example, who deliberately smashes an old record of no special interest is likely to receive a milder verbal blast than one who accidentally breaks his father's favorite record. In such cases we revert to judging the "badness" of an action in terms of material damage done rather than in terms of intention. In mental growth by substitution, therefore, there is always the possibility of a reversion to an earlier level of mental functioning.

Piaget's initial findings regarding the evolution of

mental growth and the principles of integration and substitution were not well received. His method of talking to children about a particular topic was widely criticized, his results were questioned, and his interpretations were ridiculed and dismissed. In America, as recently as ten years ago, Piaget was seen as a quaint old man who sat around on the shores of Swiss lakes talking to children about nature and the physical world.

In spite of the unfavorable reaction, Piaget persevered, extending his investigations to the study of infants—particularly his own three children—and adolescents. In this work, carried out during the 1930s and 1940s, he concerned himself mainly with the phenomena of "conservation," which in Piaget's vocabulary refers to the child's awareness that a quantity remains the same—that is, the quantity is "conserved" —despite a change in its appearance. In the example of the orangeade being poured from one size container into another, a child who recognizes that the quantity stays the same is said to "have" conservation.

What Piaget discovered during this second phase of his work was the widespread absence of quantity conservation in young children. Before the age of five or six, for example, most children believe that six pennies in a pile are fewer than six in a row, and that if one of two identical clay balls is rolled into a sausage, it increases in mass, weight, and volume. By seven or eight, however, children recognize that a change in appearance does not mean a change in amount. Piaget argued that the child's discovery of conservation in the realm of quantity was the reflection of new mental structures and new modes of organizing experience.

During this period a second principle of mental growth became evident; namely, that the emergence of new mental structures for organizing experience is accompanied by an increased ability to distinguish between appearance and reality, between how things look and how they really are. Once again, this principle of mental growth parallels what has occurred in history. Early man believed that the sun circled the earth and that the earth was flat. Such ideas come from an uncritical acceptance of information received through the senses: the sun does appear to move around the earth, and the land about us does appear flat.

We overcome the deceptive appearances of things with the aid of reason. It is the appearance of reasoning in the child that enables him to discover the conservation of quantity, number, and length. To demonstrate that reasoning is, in fact, involved, consider the following situation. Suppose an adult is presented with a clay ball and a clay sausage and asked whether they are the same weight. Without actually weighing the two objects he would have no way of knowing, but if he knew that the clay sausage had previously been a ball, and that as a ball it had been equal in weight to the other clay ball, the weight equality of ball and sausage could easily be deduced.

It is with the emergence of elementary reasoning structures, at about six or seven, that the child begins to distinguish between how things look and how they really are. But at this age his ability is limited to material things—the conservation of the length of sticks, the number of elements in a group, or the amount of liquid poured from one container into another. There remains another level at which the distinction between appearance and reality is still closed to the child; that is, the symbolic level—the level of metaphor, illusion, and double entendre.

Piaget found that it is only during adolescence that human beings become capable of making such distinctions. For example, children cannot grasp the satirical significance of political cartoons or the metaphorical significance of proverbs; only during adolescence, when still more new mental structures and mental organizations appear, do young people begin to appreciate the double meanings, the social significance, of books like *Gulliver's Travels* and *Alice in Wonderland.* Adolescents can also use irony and metaphor to belittle their enemies; they become skilled in making the apparently innocent yet cutting remark.

Thus Piaget's findings demonstrated two levels of distinction between appearance and reality: the concrete level, at which reason enables the child to discover that quantities do not change despite a change in appearance, and the symbolic level, at which adolescents discover the multifaceted meanings implicit in words and learn that the apparent meaning of words may mask their real meaning and intent. Although much of this research was done in the thirties and

forties, it did not become widely known until the late
fifties, when the *Zeitgeist* once again affected the
reception of Piaget's work.

Even before sputnik, critics of education in
America had begun to demand that educators aban-
don the goal of achieving the "personal adjustment of
the whole child" and devote themselves to teaching
children "how to think." This new emphasis led to a
search for new curricula and curricular materials.
When curriculum builders turned to psychology for
information about how the mind grows and how children think, they found that the psychologists had
little to offer. In their zeal to keep psychology a
strictly experimental science, psychological researchers had performed most of their work on learning
with lower organisms, and the results were hardly
applicable to the kind of learning that children in
school were engaged in.

It was through the efforts of men like Jerome
Bruner at Harvard, and the late David Rapaport at
the Austen Riggs Center in Stockbridge, Massa-
chusetts, that Piaget's work first came to the attention of curriculum builders. In Piaget's books educators read about the child's view of space, time, and
numbers, about children's reasoning processes and
their ability to classify and relate things. The curriculum planners discovered that Piaget had been
studying how *children* learn, and that he had come
to define learning in a new way, a way they tried to
incorporate (not always successfully) into their new
curricula.

Traditional psychology had always defined learning as "the modification of behavior as the result of experience."

Such a definition makes the learner a more or less passive recipient of environmental happenings. While this may be true of rats, it is certainly not true of children. Piaget turned the definition around and spoke of learning as, in part, "the modification of experience as the result of behavior." He argued that the child's actions upon the world changed the nature of his experience. This is another way of stating the relativity of nature and nurture. If experience is always a product (to some extent) of the child's behavior, any modification of behavior as a result of experience must be relative to the child's actions. Human experience, then, must be relative to human action.

This theory has been one of the most difficult for American educators and psychologists to accept, even those who are sympathetic to Piaget's views. It has been difficult to accept because of a lack of familiarity with Piaget's third principle of mental growth. Our tradition has been one of empiricism, which assumes a complete separation of mind and reality. Implicit in empiricism is a kind of "copy" theory of learning that says that our minds simply copy what exists in the outside world, much as a photograph copies the light patterns conveyed to the exposed film. Piaget argues that the mind never copies reality but instead organizes it and transforms it, reality, in and of itself, being—as Kant made clear—unknowable.

Everyone has had the experience of looking at the

clouds drifting by and seeing in them castles, horses, airplanes, and the like. Since different people see different things in the same cloud pattern, it is apparent that what is being seen is a product of the individual's own organizing processes. This is the principle upon which the Rorschach inkblot test is based: inkblots provide an ambiguous configuration, which allows individuals to reveal the organizing patterns of their minds.

Now, a characteristic of all such organizing activities is that the person is unaware of his own part in constructing what he sees; this is Piaget's third principle of mental growth. Many a patient confronting an inkblot has accused the examiner of showing him "dirty pictures." What Piaget has shown is that our role in organizing experience is much larger than we realize, and is a major cause of misunderstanding between adults and children. When an adult watches a quantity of liquid being poured from a short, wide container into a tall, narrow one, his organizing and deductive processes are so rapid that he literally *sees* that the quantity in the taller container is the same as it was before. The equality seems to be a property of the liquid, like its fluidity or its wetness, and to have nothing to do with his own mental processes. Yet the difficulty this problem presents to the young child shows that this awareness arises from the reasoning ability of the subject, and not from perceptible attributes of the object.

The adult actually sees the world around him in a very different way from a child who does not have conservation, but the adult is not aware of this. It is because we adults take for granted that children see the world as we do that we are often upset and angered by their behavior, and it is also the reason children often find adults unpredictable and incomprehensible. The same holds true in education, and teachers often make erroneous assumptions about how children view the world.

Piaget's fourth principle of mental growth, which is just coming to be appreciated in America, concerns motivation. On the basis of their work in animal learning, in which external rewards are required to train an animal in certain behaviors, psychologists assumed that the same held true for all learning. One of the main reasons grades are used in school, for example, is that they provide children with rewards for achievement. Children, particularly middle-class children, work hard to get good grades.

Not all learning has to be rewarded from without, however, and the structures Piaget describes lead to a kind of spontaneous learning that does not require any special rewards. If, on a certain day, one asks an adult what he has done since breakfast that morning, he will be able to give a fairly good account of his activities: though he does not set out to "remember" his activities as he might, say, a poem, and though no rewards are provided for remembering what has occurred, learning has obviously been going on. It is, however, a different kind of learning than memorizing a poem or the date of a historical incident.

Three aspects of this kind of learning should be noted. First, it involves the organization of material into a spatial or temporal or causal sequence. Second, the person is not conscious of the fact that he is processing or organizing the material. Third, and most important, such learning always involves the subject's own activity. These features of what might be called "structural learning" are present not only when we recall how we spent the morning but also in the child's attainment of the conservation of quantity and number and in his understanding of classes and logical relations. In each case the learning involves some logical ordering of information, is unconscious as far as the learner is concerned, and involves the learner's own activities, including mental activities such as reasoning.

Accordingly, it is not really appropriate to ask "why" a child attains conservation in the same way that we might ask "why" he knocked his brother down. The latter question presupposes conscious intention and demands an "answer" in dynamic terms: the reply could be "his brother hit him," or "his brother took his toy," or something to that effect. It is an entirely different matter to ask why a child has *not* attained conservation. The question is analogous to asking "why doesn't a fish walk?" In both cases an intentional answer is inappropriate. To say that the child does not attain conservation because he is too lazy or too busy with other things is like saying that a fish doesn't walk because it prefers to swim. For both questions the appropriate answer is one of structure and function.

To explain why a fish swims you must describe the

natural history of the fish, the structure and shape of its body and gills, and the functioning of its breathing apparatus. Likewise, to explain why a child attains conservation, his mental structures and their functions must be described. If a fish cannot walk, it is because it lacks the necessary physical structures, and if a child has not attained conservation, then, other things being equal, he must lack the necessary mental structures. Conservation is thus as natural a function of elementary reasoning abilities as swimming is a natural function of the fish's organs and body conformation.

It is because Piaget stresses this sort of "motivation" that he has spent a good part of his career in formulating in more specific terms the mental structures that characterize the development of intelligence from infancy through adolescence. Piaget has described four stages of mental growth, which he summarizes in terms of the major cognitive task each seems designed to accomplish. During the first two years of life (the sensory-motor period) the mental structures are mainly concerned with the mastery of concrete objects. The second stage, from about two to six or seven (the preoperational period), concerns the mastery of symbols, including those that occur in language, fantasy, play, and dreams. During the third stage, from about six or seven to about twelve (the concrete operational period), children learn the mastery of classes, relations, and numbers and how to reason about them. Finally, from about twelve to fifteen (the formal operational period),

young people are concerned with the mastery of
thought and can think about their own and other
people's thinking.

These stages of mental growth, and the principles
manifested in their development, are gradually im-
pressing themselves on American psychology and
education but not always in undistorted form. Now
that Piaget's name has become well known, it is
often invoked in support of many viewpoints and
practices that are in opposition to the real direction
of Piaget's work. Piaget, for example, is cited as an
authority by those who advocate formal preschool
instruction for young children *and* by those who
argue for the value of play and informal methods of
education for young children. Piaget is both criticized
for views he does not hold and praised for positions
he has never taken.

In 1969 the American Psychological Association
presented Piaget with an award for his distinguished
contribution to psychology. Despite this formal rec-
ognition, Piaget retains the ambiguous position of
the intellectual innovator. It will probably be decades
before his ideas become firmly rooted within the
canons of psychology, and then Piaget, like Freud,
will be dismissed because the valuable part of his
work will have become part of the established modes
of psychological thought. Piaget knows this, but he
has always had the indifference to fame, the independence of mind, the steadfastness of purpose, and
the dedication to truth that mark the true intellectual
innovator. And though Piaget has not always been

treated generously by his colleagues, he retains his sense of humor, his pleasure in work, his wonder at the world, and his delight in people. Not the least of Piaget's contributions is the example he provides to his students and, indeed, to all young people, of a life well lived in the service of science and mankind.

PART C: *Genetic Epistemology by Jean Piaget*

Genetic epistemology deals with the formation and meaning of knowledge and with the means by which the human mind goes from a lower level of knowledge to one that is judged to be higher. It is not for psychologists to decide what knowledge is lower or higher but rather to explain how the transition is made from one to the other. The nature of these transitions is a factual matter. They are historical, or psychological, or sometimes even biological.

The fundamental hypothesis of genetic epistemology is that there is a parallelism between the progress made in the logical and rational organization of knowledge and the corresponding formative psychological processes. With that hypothesis, the most fruitful, most obvious field of study would be the reconstituting of human history—the history of human thinking in prehistoric man. Unfortunately, we are not very well informed in the psychology of primitive man, but there are children all around us, and it is in studying children that we have the best chance of studying the development of logical knowledge, mathematical knowledge, physical knowledge, and so forth.

When we consider the nature of knowledge, the use of psychological data is indispensable. All epistemologists refer to psychological factors in their analyses but, for the most part, such references are speculative and not based on psychological research. Unfortunately for psychology, everybody thinks of himself as a psychologist. When an epistemologist needs to consider some psychological aspect of a problem, he does not refer to psychological research and he does not consult psychologists; he depends on his own reflections. He puts together certain ideas and relations within his own thinking. Logical positivists, in particular, have never taken psychology into account in their epistemology. They affirm that logical and mathematical reality are derived from language. Here it becomes necessary to look at factual findings, at the logical behavior in children before language develops.

In my discussion of the development of logical structures in children, I should like to start by making a distinction between two complementary aspects of thought: the figurative and the operative. The figurative aspect is an imitation of states taken as momentary and static. In the cognitive area the figurative functions are, above all, perception, imitation, and mental imagery, which is interiorized imitation. The operative aspect deals not with states but with transformations from one state to another. It includes actions themselves, which transform objects or states, and intellectual operations, which are essentially systems of transformation. The figurative aspects are always subordinated to the operative. Any state can be understood only as the result of certain transformations, or as the point of departure for other transformations. To me, therefore, the essential aspect of thought is its operative aspect; I think that human knowledge is essentially active. To know is to assimilate reality into systems of transformation. To know is to transform reality in order to understand how a certain state is brought about.

By virtue of this point of view, I find myself opposed to the view of knowledge as a passive copy of reality. In point of fact, this notion is based on a vicious circle: in order to make a copy you have to know the model you are copying, but the only way you know the model is by copying it. I believe, however, that knowing an object means acting upon it, constructing systems of transformations that can be carried out on or with this object. Knowing reality means constructing systems of transformations that correspond, more or less adequately, to reality. They are more or less isomorphic to transformations of reality. The transformational structures of which knowledge consists are not copies of the transformations in reality; they are simply possible isomorphic models among which experience can enable us to choose. Knowledge, then, is a system of transformations that become progressively adequate.

It is agreed that logical and mathematical structures are abstract, while physical knowledge, which is based on experience, is concrete. But let us ask what logical and mathematical knowledge is abstracted from. There are two possibilities. The first is that when we act upon an object our knowledge is derived from the object itself. A child, for instance, can heft objects in his hands and realize that they have different weights—that usually big things weigh more than little things, but that sometimes little things weigh more than big things. All this he finds out experientially, and his knowledge is abstracted from the objects themselves. This is the point of view of empiricism in general, and it is true for the most part in the case of experimental or empirical knowledge. But there is a second possibility: when we are acting upon an object we can also take into account the action itself, or operation, since the transformation can be carried out mentally. In this hypothesis, the abstraction is drawn not from the object acted upon, but from the action itself. It seems to me that this is the basis of logical and mathematical abstraction. Here I should like to give an example, one we have studied quite thoroughly with a lot of children. It was first suggested to me by a mathematician friend who quoted it as the point of departure of his interest in mathematics. When he was a small child he was counting pebbles one day; he lined them up in a row and counted them from left to right and got to ten. Then, just for fun, he counted them from right to left to see what he would get, and was astonished that he got ten again. He put the

pebbles in a circle and counted them and once again
there were ten. He went around the circle the other
way and got ten again. And no matter how he put the
pebbles, when he counted them they came to ten.
He discovered here what is known in mathematics as
commutativity; that is, the sum is independent of the
order. But how did he discover this? Was commutativity a property of the pebbles? It is true that the
pebbles, as it were, let it be done to themselves; he
could not have done the same thing with drops of
water. So in this sense there was a physical aspect to
his knowledge. But the order was not in the pebbles;
it was he, the subject, who put the pebbles in a line
and then in a circle. Moreover, the sum was not in the
pebbles themselves; it was he who united the pebbles.
The knowledge that this future mathematician discovered that day was drawn, then, not from the physical
properties of the pebbles, but from the actions that he
carried out on them.

The first type of abstraction from objects I shall
refer to as "simple abstraction"; the second type I
shall call "reflective abstraction," using this term in
a double sense. "Reflective" here has a meaning in
psychology in addition to the one it has in physics. In
its physical sense reflection refers to such phenomena
as the reflection of a beam of light off one surface onto
another surface. In this sense the abstraction is a reflection from the level of action to the intellectual
level of operation. On the other hand, reflection refers
to the mental process of reflection; that is, at the level
of thought a reorganization takes place.

I should like now to make a distinction between two

types of actions. On the one hand, there are individual actions—like throwing, pushing, touching, rubbing. It is these actions that usually give rise to abstraction from the objects. This is the simple abstraction I discussed above. Reflective abstraction, however, is based not on individual actions but on coordinated action. Actions can be coordinated in different ways. They can be joined together (additive coordination); they can succeed each other in a temporal order (ordinal or sequential coordination); a correspondence between one action and another can be set up; or intersections among actions can be established. All these forms of coordination have parallels in logical structures, and it is this coordination at the level of action that seems to me to be at the basis of logical structures as they develop later in thought. This, in fact, is my hypothesis: that the roots of logical thought are not to be found in language alone, even though language coordinations are important. Rather, the roots of logic are to be found more generally in the coordination of actions, which are the basis of reflective abstraction.

This is only the beginning of a regressive analysis that could go much further. In genetic epistemology, as in developmental psychology, there is never an absolute beginning. We can never get back to the point where we can say, here is the very beginning of logical structures. As soon as we start talking about the general coordination of actions, we find ourselves going even further into biology, which is not my intention here. I just want to carry this regressive analysis back to its beginnings in psychology and emphasize again that the formation of logical and mathematical structures in human thinking cannot be explained by language alone, but has its roots in the general co-ordination of actions.

The decisive argument against the position that logical mathematical structures are derived uniquely from linguistic forms is that in the course of any individual's intellectual development, logical mathematical structures exist *before* the appearance of language. Language appears somewhere about the middle of the second year, but before then, about the end of the first year or the beginning of the second, there is a sensory-motor intelligence that is a practical intelligence having its own logic—a logic of action. The actions that form sensory-motor intelligence are capable of being repeated and of being generalized. For example, a child who has learned to pull a blanket toward him in order to reach a toy that is on it is then capable of pulling the blanket to reach anything else that may be placed on it. The action can also be generalized so that he learns to pull a string to reach what is attached to the end of the string, or so that he can use a stick to move a distant object. Whatever is repeatable and generalizable in an action is what I have called a scheme, and I maintain that there is a logic of schemes. Any given scheme in itself does not have a logical component, but schemes can be coordinated with one another, thus implying the general coordination of actions. These coordinations form a logic of actions that are the point of departure for the logical mathematical structures. For example, a scheme can consist of subschemes or sub-systems. If I move a stick to move an object, there is within that scheme one subscheme of the relation between the hand and the stick, a second subscheme of the relation between the stick and the object, a third subscheme of the relation between the object and its position in space, and so on. This is the beginning of the relation of inclusion. The subschemes are included within the total scheme, just as in the logical mathematical structure of classification subclasses are included within the total class. At a later stage this relation of class inclusion gives rise to concepts. At the sensory-motor stage a scheme is a sort of practical concept.

Another type of logic involved in the coordination of schemes is the logic of order: for instance, to achieve an end we have to go through certain means. There is thus an order between the means and the goal. Once again, it is practical-order relations of this sort that are the basis of the later logical mathematical structures of order. There is also a primitive type of one-to-one correspondence. When an infant imitates a model, there is a correspondence between the model on the one hand and his imitation on the other. Even when he imitates himself, that is, when he repeats an action, there is a correspondence between the action as carried out one time and the action as carried out the next.

In other words, we find in sensory-motor intelligence a certain logic of inclusion, a certain logic of ordering, and a certain logic of correspondence, which I maintain are the foundations for logical mathematical structures. They are certainly not operations, but they are the beginnings of what will later become operations. We can also find in this sensory-motor intelligence the beginnings of two essential characteristics of operations, namely, a form of conservation and a form of reversibility.

The conservation characteristic of sensory-motor intelligence takes the form of the notion of the permanence of an object. This notion does not exist until near the end of the infant's first year. If a seven- or eight-month-old reaches for an object that interests him and we suddenly put a screen between him and the object, not only has the object disappeared but it also is no longer accessible. He will withdraw his hand and make no attempt to push aside the screen, even if it is as delicate a screen as a handkerchief. Near the end of the first year, however, he will push aside the screen and continue to reach for the object. He will even be able to keep track of a successive number of changes of position. If the object is put in a box and the box is put behind a chair, for instance, the child will be able to follow these successive changes of position. This notion of the permanence of an object, then, is the sensory-motor equivalent of the notions of conservation that develop later at the operational level.

Similarly, we can see the beginnings of reversibility in the understanding of spatial positions and changes of position. At the beginning of the second year, children have a practical notion of space which geometers call the group of displacements, that is, the understanding that a movement in one direction can be canceled by a movement in another direction—that a point in space can be reached by one of a number of different routes. This, of course, is the detour behavior that psychologists have studied in such detail in chimpanzees and infants.

This, again, is practical intelligence. It is not at the level of thought, and it is not at all representational, but the child can act in space with this intelligence. Furthermore, this organization exists as early as the second half of the first year, before any use of language for expression. So much for my first argument.

My second argument deals with children whose thinking is logical but who do not have language available to them, namely, the deaf and dumb. Before I discuss the experimental findings on intelligence in deaf-and-dumb children, I should like to discuss briefly the nature of representation. Between the ages of about eighteen months and seven or eight years, when the operations appear, the practical logic of sensory-motor intelligence goes through a period of being internalized, of taking shape in thought at the level of representation rather than in the carrying out of actions only. I should like to insist here on a point that is too often forgotten: there are many forms of representation. Actions can be represented in a number of different ways, of which language is only one. It is merely one aspect of the general function that some call the symbolic function. I prefer to use the linguistics term and call it the semiotic function. This is the ability to represent something by a sign or a symbol or another object. In addition to language, the semiotic function includes gestures, either idiosyncratic or, as in the case of the deaf-and-dumb language, systematized. It includes deferred imitation, that is, imitation that takes place when the model is no longer present. It includes drawing, painting, modeling, and mental imagery, or internalized imitation. In all these there is a signifier representing that which is signified, and all these ways are used by individual children in their passage from intelligence that is acted out to intelligence that is thought. Language is but one among many aspects of the semiotic function, even though it is in most instances the most important.

This position is confirmed by the fact that in deaf-and-dumb children we find thought without language and logical structures without language. Professor Pierre Oleron in France has done interesting work in this area. In the United States I should like to mention especially the work of Hans Furth and his excellent book, *Thinking Without Language*. Furth finds a certain delay in the development of logical structures in deaf-and-dumb children as compared with normal children. This is not surprising since the social stimulation of the former is so limited, but apart from this delay the development of the logical structures is similar. He finds classifications of the sort discussed before; he finds correspondence; he finds numerical quantity; and he finds the representation of space. In short, there is well-developed logical thinking in these children even without language.

Another interesting point is that although deaf-and-dumb children are delayed compared to normal children, they are delayed much less than children who have been blind from birth. Blind infants have the great disadvantage of not being able to make the same coordinations in space that normal children are capable of during the first year or two, so that the development of sensory-motor intelligence and the coordination of actions at this level are seriously impeded in blind children. For this reason we find that there are even greater delays in their development at the level of representational thinking and that language is not sufficient to compensate for the deficiency in the coordination of actions. The delay is made up ultimately, of course, but it is significant and considerably more than the delay in the development of logic in deaf-and-dumb children.

My final argument will be based on the work of Madame Hermine Sinclair, who studied the relations between operational and linguistic levels in children between the ages of five and eight years. Mme. Sinclair was a linguist before coming to study psychology in Geneva; at her first contact with our work she was convinced of the logical positivist position, that is, that the operational level of children simply reflected their linguistic level. I suggested to her that she study this question, since it had never been studied closely, and see what relations existed between the two. As a result, Mme. Sinclair performed the following experiment: first she established two groups of children. One group consisted of conservers—those who realized that when liquid was poured from a glass of one shape into a glass of another shape the quantity did not change, in spite of appearances. The other group consisted of nonconservers—those who judged the quantity of liquid according to its appearance and not according to any correlation between height and width of container, or reasoning in terms of the fact that no liquid had been added or taken away. Then Mme. Sinclair proceeded to study the language of each group by giving them very simple objects to describe. Usually she presented the objects in pairs so that the children could describe them by comparing them as well as citing their individual characteristics. (She gave them, for instance, pencils of different widths and lengths.) She found noticeable differences in the language used to describe these objects according to whether the child was a conserver or a nonconserver. Nonconservers tended to describe objects in terms that linguists call "scalers." That is, they would describe one object at a time and one characteristic at a time—"That pencil is long"; "That pencil is fat"; "It is short"; etc. The conservers, on the other hand, used what linguists call "vectors." They would keep in mind both objects at once and more than one characteristic at once. They would say, "This pencil is longer than that one, but that one is fatter than this one"—sentences of that sort.

So far the experiment seemed to show a relation between the operational level and the linguistic level, but it did not indicate in what sense the influence is exercised. Is the linguistic level influencing the operational level, or is the operational level influencing the linguistic progress? To find the answer Mme. Sinclair went on to another aspect of the experiment. She gave linguistic training to the nonconserving group. Through classical learning-theory methods, she taught these children to describe the objects in the same terms that the conservers used. Then she examined them again to see whether this training had affected their operational level. (She did this experiment in several areas of operations, not only for conservation but also for seriation and other areas.) In every case she found that there was only minimal progress after the linguistic training. Only ten percent of the children advanced from one substage to another. This is such a small percentage that it leads one to wonder whether these children were not already at an intermediate phase and right on the threshold of the next substage. Mme. Sinclair's conclusion, on the basis of these experiments, is that intellectual operations appear to give rise to linguistic progress, not vice versa.

I should like to go on now to examine the type of thinking that children are capable of in what I call the preoperational stage, that is, ages four, five, and six, before the development of logical operations. Although logical structures are not fully developed at this stage, we can find there what I once called "articulated intuitions," but now, after a good deal more research, I would call, very literally, "semilogic." That is, the thought of children of these ages is characterized by half-logic, or operations that lack reversibility; they work only in one direction. This logic consists of functions as described by mathematicians: $y = (f)x$. A function in this sense represents an ordered couple or an application, but one that moves always in one direction. This kind of thinking leads to

the discovery of dependent relations and covaria-
tions: the correlation of variations in one object with
variations in another.

The remarkable thing about these functions is that
they do not lead to conservation. Here is one example:
a piece of string, attached to a small spring, goes out
horizontally, around a pivot, and hangs down vertically. Now, when we put a weight, or increase the
weight, on the end of the string, the string is pulled
so that the part hanging vertically is lengthened compared to the horizontal part. Five-year-olds are perfectly capable of grasping that with the greater
weight the vertical part is longer and the horizontal
is shorter, and further that when the vertical part
becomes shorter the horizontal becomes longer. But
they do not thereby become conservationists. For
them, the sum of the vertical and horizontal parts
does not stay the same.

Here is another example of a function in the sense
of an application. Children are given a number of
cards, on each of which there is a white part and a
red part, and they are given cutouts of different
shapes. Their task is to find the cutout that will
cover up the red part on the card. It need not correspond exactly, but it must cover the card so that no
red part shows. The interesting thing is that these
children understand the relation many-to-one—they
realize that a number of the different cutout shapes
can cover the red. Nevertheless, they do not go on
from there to construct a classification system based
on the relation of one-to-many. Once again, it is a
case of half of a logical structure.

More generally, the reason why functions are so interesting is that they show us clearly the importance of relations of order in preoperational thinking. Many relations that are metric for us are simply ordinal for children: measure does not enter into their judgments. A good illustration is the conservation of length. If two sticks are the same length when they are side by side, we would judge them to be the same length when they are separated because we would take into account both ends and realize that the important thing is the distance between the left and right ends in each case. Preoperational children, however, do not base their judgments on the order of the end points. If they are looking at one end of the stick their judgments of length are based on which one goes further in that direction.

Another characteristic of semilogic is the notion of identity, which precedes the notion of conservation. We have already seen that there is a certain notion of identity in sensory-motor intelligence; a child realizes that an object has a certain permanence. This is not conservation in the sense that we have been using the term, since the object does not change its form in any way, but only its position. Yet, it is identity, and one of the starting points for the later notion of conservation. In our studies of the notion of identity in preoperational thinking from the age of about four years, we have found that it is highly variable. What it means for something to preserve its identity changes according to the age of the child and according to the situation in which the problem is presented.

The first thing to keep in mind is that identity is a

qualitative, not a quantitative notion. For instance, a preoperational child who will maintain that the quantity of water changes according to the shape of its container, will nonetheless affirm that it is the same water—only the quantity has changed. My colleague, Jerome Bruner, thinks that a notion of the principle of identity is sufficient as a foundation for the notion of conservation. But I find this position questionable. To have the principle of identity one has only to distinguish between that which changes in a given transformation and that which does not change. In the case of the pouring of liquids, children need only make a distinction between the form and the substance. But more than that is required in the notion of conservation. Quantification is rather more complex, especially since the most primitive quantitative notions are the ordinal ones, which are not adequate in all cases of quantitative comparison. It is not until children also develop the operation of compensation and reversibility that the quantitative notion of conservation is established.

Now I should like to go on to some new examples of how the notion of identity changes with development. We have done several different experiments and found a first level where identity is semi-individual and semigeneric. A child will believe that objects are identical to the extent that one can do the same things with them. For instance, a collection of beads on a table is recognized as being the same as the beads in the form of a necklace, because one can take them apart and make a pile of them or string them together into a necklace. Similarly, a piece of wire in the shape of an arc is recognized as being the same when it is straight, because it can be bent into an arc or pulled into a straight line. A little later a child becomes more demanding in his criteria for identity, however. Then it is no longer sufficient that the object be assimilated to a certain scheme. The identity becomes more individualized. At this stage he will say that it is no longer the same piece of wire when it is in the shape of an arc, because it no longer has the same form.

One interesting experiment illustrating this grew out of another experiment. Children were ordering squares according to size, and in the course of this activity one child put a square on a corner instead of along the edge, and then he rejected it, saying that it was no longer a square. We then started another experiment in which we investigated this more closely, presenting a cutout square in different positions and asking questions like the following: Is it the same square? Is it still a square? Is it the same piece of cardboard? Are the sides still the same length? Are the diagonals still the same length? We put these questions, of course, in terms that made sense to the children we were interviewing. We found that until the age of about seven the children denied the identity. They insisted that it was no longer the same square, that it was no longer a square at all, that the sides were no longer the same length, and so on.

Similar experiments are possible in the area of perception. We are all familiar with the phenomenon of apparent or stroboscopic motion. One object appears and disappears, and as it disappears, another appears,

and as the second object disappears, the first appears
again. If this is done at the right speed it looks as if
the same object is moving back and forth between two
positions. It occurred to me that it would be interesting to study the phenomenon of identity through the
phenomenon of stroboscopic motion by having one of
the objects a circle and the other a square—so when
the object moves to one side it looks as if it is becoming a circle, and when it moves to the other side it
looks as if it is becoming a square. It looks like a single
object that is changing its shape as it changes its
position. I should point out that it is much easier for
children to see this apparent motion than it is for
adults. But the interesting thing in our experiment is
that despite their facility in seeing stroboscopic motion, the children tend to deny the identity of the object. They will say that it is a circle until it gets almost
to the other side, and then it becomes a square; or,
that it is no longer the same object—one takes the
place of the other. Adults, on the other hand, see a
circle that turns into a square, and a square that turns
into a circle. They find it strange, but nonetheless,
that is what they see. It is the same object changing
its shape. According to this experiment, then, the
notion of identity increases with age. And this is only
one of many experiments in which we have found
similar results.

One last experiment I should like to mention was
carried out by Voyat on the growth of the plant.
Voyat started by experimenting with the growth of
a bean plant, but that took too long, so he turned to a
chemical solution that grows in a few minutes into

an arborescent shape that looks something like sea-weed. As a child watches this plant grow he is period-ically asked to draw it; then, with his drawings as reminders, he is asked if at the various points in its growth it is still the same plant. We use whatever term the child uses to refer to it—a plant, seaweed, macaroni, or whatever. Then we ask him to draw himself when he was a baby, when he was a little bigger, a little bigger than that, and as he is now. And we ask the same questions as to whether all these drawings are of the same person, whether it is always he. At a relatively young age, a child will deny that the same plant is represented in his various drawings. In referring to the drawings of himself, however, he will likely say that it is the same person. Then if we go back to the drawings of the plant, some children will be influenced by their thoughts on their drawings of themselves and say that now they realize that it is the same plant. But others will continue to deny that it is the same plant, maintaining that it has changed too much, that it is a different plant now. Here, then, is an amusing experiment that shows that the changes that take place within the logical thinking of children as they grow older affect the notion of identity itself. Even identity changes in this field of continual transformation and change.

DIALOGUE
WITH

JEAN
PIAGET

REACTIONS TO PSYCHOANALYSIS AND OTHER BASIC CONCEPTS AND VIEWS IN PSYCHOLOGY

PART I

Overview | In this section I attempt to obtain Piaget's reaction to a number of the fundamental concepts dealt with in many of our introductory psychology books. Piaget reacts to such Freudian ideas as the unconscious and psychosexual development. He also reacts to Erik Erikson's views of psychosocial development and the notion of the importance of loving the child. He expresses his views concerning the traditional homeostatic model of motivation (that needs create tensions and that most behavior is directed at tension reduction), learning theory, perception, and the Gestalt school of psychology.

EVANS: To begin our discussion, Dr. Piaget, we have always thought it rather interesting to get the reaction of our distinguished interviewees to psychoanalytic theory. We know, of course, that you have had contact with several aspects of the psychoanalytic movement. You might begin by telling us a little bit about the extent of your contact with some of the leaders of the psychoanalytic movement.

PIAGET: I knew Freud at the 1922 Congress of Psychoanalysis in Berlin. I gave a lecture at this Congress and I remember the anxiety I felt as a lecturer in front of a large audience. Freud was seated to my right in an armchair smoking his cigars, and I was addressing the public, but the public never glanced at their lecturer. They looked only at Freud, to find out whether or not he was happy with what was being said. When Freud smiled, everybody in the room smiled; when Freud looked serious, everybody in the room looked serious.

But that is just being light. In

fact, I have learned a lot from psychoanalysis. This psychodynamic point of view completely renovated psychology. But I think that the future of psychoanalysis will be the day it becomes experimental, as Rapaport and his students such as Wolfe have already started to do. Until it becomes experimental, as long as it simply remains at the level of discussion of clinical cases, it is not entirely convincing in all of its detail.

EVANS: How do you feel about Freud's concept of the unconscious?

PIAGET: I think that the concept of the unconscious itself is completely general; it is not at all restricted to the emotional life. In any area of cognitive functioning, all the processes are unconscious. We are conscious of the result, not of the mechanism. When we take cognizance of our processes, we start from the periphery and go from there towards the heart of the mechanism, but we never get there entirely. The emotional unconscious is therefore a special case of the unconscious in general; and this is whatever cannot be made clearly explicit, because of an absence of reflective abstraction, conceptualization, etc. The unconscious is whatever is not conceptualized.

EVANS: In this respect, a very important part of this whole theory was Freud's development of the psychosexual model. As you know, he felt that during the first five years of life the child and infant pass through a number of biologically determined stages, each of which is designed to cope with various areas of premature sexuality and its gratification. He felt that the patterns that developed during the first five years of life such as the so-called Oedipal situation pretty much formed the basis for all later relationships.

How do you feel about this theory of psychosexual development that Freud postulated?

PIAGET: Ah, there are two questions. I do not think that the initial stages determine everything to come. I think the truth is rather the way Erikson (Evans, 1969) sees it—the past determines the present, but the present acts upon our interpretation of the past, so that the past is always interpreted in terms of the present situation; there is interaction between the present and the past.

Now as for Freud's stages, what is troublesome is that they are essentially determined by a predominant characteristic. The stage does not have a total structure, it simply has a dominant characteristic. And obviously it is always a rather subjective matter to decide whether or not a characteristic is dominant. One particular study has been done of the relationship between Freudian stages and cognitive stages by a Canadian psychologist, Madame Gouin Décarie (1965). She took up my experiments on the development of object permanency in babies and she tried to relate them to the Freudian notion of object relations. There is a clear relationship, certainly—she was able to show this. But the main point of interest in this study is that she was able to distinguish ten steps in my stages of development of object permanency and was able to verify these ten steps in each of the ninety babies she studied; while the steps that she distinguished in the Freudian stages did not show the same

constancy—among the ninety babies there were
changes in the order in which these steps appeared.
This indicates that the notion of a predominant characteristic is not precise enough yet. But psychoanalysis
in general has to become more experimental. If it is
simply a school where everyone believes what the
other is saying—well, truth that is acquired this way
is dangerous.

EVANS: You just referred to object permanency.
Could you elaborate a bit on the meaning of the concept?

PIAGET: It is the idea that even outside the child's
perceptual field, an object continues to exist. By contrast during the child's first few months, if an object
leaves his perceptual field, he shows no indication
that he is looking for it. Even if he is reaching out for
it with his hands, and you put a screen over it to hide
it from his view, he withdraws his hands as if the
object did not exist any longer. By object permanency
I mean simply the fact that an object continues to
exist even when it has left the perceptual field.

EVANS: Getting back to Freudian theory, Erikson
also tried to parallel Freud's *psychosexual* development with a process of *psychosocial* development,
feeling that at the same time that we have a series
of biological developments in the individual there are
also some very important psychosocial developments
which have to do with the development of values and
character and personality.

PIAGET: Oh, I am convinced that is fundamental.
It is impossible to disassociate the biological and the
social aspects when you are dealing with psychologi-

cal development. A phenomenon is always biological in its roots, and social at its end point. But we must not forget, also, that between the two it is mental.

EVANS: One of the important derivatives of psychoanalytic theory in the contemporary scene seems to be the importance of love. We have the work of Bowlby (1969) and Spitz (1965) and others who demonstrate that without this very fundamental love early in the development of the child, the child will actually deteriorate physiologically. Do you feel stressing this great need that the child has for love is an important consideration in studying development?

PIAGET: I have no idea about love, but affectivity certainly is central. Affectivity is the motor of any conduct. But affectivity does not modify the cognitive structure. Take two school children for example. One who loves mathematics, who is interested and enthusiastic, and anything else you wish; and the other who has feelings of inferiority, dislikes the teacher, and so forth. One will go much faster than the other, but for both of them two and two makes four in the end. It doesn't make three for the one who doesn't like it and five for the one who does. Two and two are still four.

EVANS: How do you view this kind of a model, this homeostatic model of motivation which is pretty much the kind of model you see in psychoanalysis and is reflected in most of our introductory psychology textbooks in the United States? This model, borrowed from physiology, represents the organism as continually responding to needs which create tensions which "demand" reduction—

PIAGET: I think this is a basic model, and it is not only in psychoanalysis and in American psychology that we find this kind of regulatory model. For instance, Pierre Janet had a theory of affectivity, of which we know all too little, in which he speaks of regulations among what he calls the elementary feelings. He is not speaking here of feelings which govern conduct between one individual and another, but of elementary feelings like effort, fatigue, the joys of success, the sadness of failures, etc. In his theory, all such feelings are regulations, and homeostasis is basic.

In cognition, as well, homeostasis is a basic model. Right throughout cognitive development, every progress is the result of a self-regulation. Moreover, I think that the notion of homeostasis, which marks the end state, must be completed by Waddington's notion of homeorhesis, or the dynamic equilibrium which characterizes the path of the development. When there is deviation from the path, self-regulations come into play to bring about a return to the path.

EVANS: Another very important part of our orientation in contemporary psychology which deals with the problem of modifying behavior is learning. As you know, learning theories go in several directions. Among these are cognitive learning theories such as the work of Tolman (1932), who emphasized the role of experiential organization in learning. On the other hand, there are models of learning that are primarily behavior oriented. This approach is currently exemplified by Skinner (Evans, 1968) and earlier was most significantly reflected in the work of the late Clark Hull (1943). Of these two general orientations to learning, cognitive versus behavioral, which would you lean toward the most, the cognitive model of Tolman or behavioral models such as Skinner's? Also, how would you relate learning to development?

PIAGET: Oh, there is no question that I feel closest to Tolman, with his meaningful indices, etc. It seems to me that there are two central questions in the problem of learning in relation to development. The first one is whether development is simply a matter of a series of learnings, or whether learning depends on what embryologists call competence, that is, the organism's possibilities. That is, is learning the fundamental thing, or is development the fundamental thing? Well, this is the very problem that B. Inhelder is currently studying, and I think we already have every proof that development is more fundamental than learning. The same learning situation has a different effect according to the stage of development of the subject.

The second question is this: Is learning simply a matter of associations which are confirmed by external reinforcements? External reinforcements do play a role of course, but they are not at all the whole story. Internal reinforcements play their role too. All of the homeostatic and self-regulatory models that we were talking about a moment ago demonstrate that external reinforcement is insufficient.

EVANS: Another theme in introductory courses in psychology centers around the term perception. What approach to perception would be most compatible with your own views?

PIAGET: Our central emphasis is to distinguish between perception as a resultant, or stabilized totality,

and perceptual activity. Perceptual activities are our
own active efforts to explore a figure, or to explore
the relationship between figures. Perceptual activity
like this has a great deal in common with intelligence.
Similar mechanisms come into play. For instance there
are mechanisms in common between perceptual con-
stancies on the one hand and operational conservations[1] or higher applications of reasoning on the
other, even though the latter appear seven or eight
years later. One problem is to try to get at what is
the common mechanism, but we also want to try to
understand why this same mechanism comes into play
so much later in the case of intelligence than in the
case of perception.

EVANS: Pursuing for a moment our discussion of
perception, Dr. Piaget, one of the things that, of
course, would be of great interest is whether you
had any contact with any of the early advocates of the
Gestalt school of psychology.[2]

PIAGET: Yes, indeed, I knew Köhler, Wertheimer,
and others, and I was very much influenced by Gestalt
theory. I think the idea of studying totalities was a
basic one. But actually I think there are three possible
points of view, and not two. There is the atomistic
approach, which starts from independent sensations

[1] Although Piaget seldom uses this exact phrase "operational
conservations" in his works, he probably intends to denote
higher-order mental acts which have the property of remaining
structurally invariant across symbolic transformations.
[2] The Gestalt school of psychology emphasized the holistic
nature of perception, that the "whole is greater than the sum of
its parts" and also discussed innate organizational tendencies
in perception.

and proceeds to build associations among these sensations. The Gestaltists destroyed this point of view. Then the Gestaltists themselves, the second point of view, start with the totality, but they take the totality to be an explanation by itself. It seems to me that leaves a serious gap. The third possible point of view, it seems to me, is to conceive of totalities in a relational way. That is, a totality is composed not of elements but of relations. Elements never are perceived alone, they are always perceived in relationships. But these relationships can be studied and we can find in this way laws of composition, among elements and relations, which generate the totalities, rather than starting with ready-made totalities like the good form. I think that the Gestalt psychologists were too much influenced by the notion of a field as it existed in physics, and particularly in electromagnetism. I believe that instead we must substitute the notion of a self-regulatory equilibrium, such as we were discussing a moment ago, and to do this we must think in terms of a relational totality and not simply a global totality with a fixed form.

STAGES OF COGNITIVE DEVELOPMENT

PART II

Overview | In this section Piaget traces his vitally important stages of cognitive development from the very beginning sensory-motor period (to two years) to the preoperational period (two to seven years), to the concrete operational period (seven to eleven years) and finally to the formal operational period (eleven to fifteen years). Of particular interest here is Piaget's discussion of such notions as imitation and awareness of the self, and his recognition of different rates of the child's development during these stages.

EVANS: I think it would be interesting to move now to something that is uniquely yours, Dr. Piaget, and this, of course, is your developmental model. As I understand your developmental model, you appear to believe that the process of knowing begins to take place before the child acquires language; therefore, starting with language is not the key: you must start before language. And this prelanguage stage you called the sensory-motor period.[1] Is this correct?

PIAGET: It is entirely correct. The sensory-motor period is extremely remarkable in development, because it is during this period, from birth to the middle of the second year, that the most fundamental and the most rapid changes take place. At birth, there are only isolated actions like sucking, touching things by accident, listening, etc. And furthermore everything is centered on the infant's own body.

[1] The sensory-motor period is the first stage of Piaget's developmental model. It is designated as the time from birth until the beginning of symbolic thought.

For the infant, objects do not exist in themselves and the infant is not conscious of itself as a subject, as Baldwin (1955) showed a long time ago. But during the first year and a half or so, a Copernican revolution takes place, in the sense that now the child's own body is no longer the center, but has become an object among other objects, and objects now are related to each other by either causal relationships, or spatial relationships, in a coherent space that englobes them all. All of these basic changes take place before there is any language, which demonstrates to what an extent knowledge is tied to actions, and not only to verbalizations.

EVANS: What would be some specific things that we would observe in this infant as it progresses from the very beginning to the end of this period? Can you give us some specific examples that would illustrate each of the substages of the sensory-motor period?

PIAGET: That would take quite a long time, because there are six substages. But as an example, let us look at one type of conduct which is one of the first clear-cut examples of sensory-motor intelligence. A child wants an object which is out of his reach, but which is resting on a blanket, and he pulls the object to him by pulling the blanket that the object is resting on. This may seem rather simple on the face of it, but it assumes a lot of relationships, and we can follow the progressive construction of each of these relationships. For example, the relationship "resting upon." This relationship is not at all obvious to an infant; to carry out the more complicated conduct, the child first had to construct that relationship. Another relationship involved here is that of moving the distant object from one place to another. The idea that it is possible to move an object with some consistency from one place to another also had to be constructed by this child. Then there is the matter of coordinating these two relationships together, by using the blanket, not quite as a tool, but as an intermediary between the child itself and the distant object. That is one example of an act of sensory-motor intelligence in which we were able to follow all the steps in the construction of the various relationships involved.

EVANS: Yes, so the child will go through a discovery process. Would that be a good word to use here?

PIAGET: "Discovery" isn't enough. We are dealing here with the construction of new relations. The relation, "resting upon," and the relationship "pull closer through the means of an intermediary," are based on all sorts of actions, movements from place to place, manipulations. I wouldn't call them discoveries. They are real inventions, because they are new constructions.

EVANS: Now one of the very tricky aspects of the sensory-motor period, which makes it very difficult to understand, is the fact that we are so accustomed to thinking in terms of language as a means of understanding. Here, Dr. Piaget, you are postulating that there is understanding without language. Since we use language to communicate, it is rather difficult to visualize what understanding without language must

be like. Is there any way that you can describe what
this must be like?

PIAGET: When there is no language there is no concept in the sense of a name for a collection of objects,
let us say. But there are already what I call "schemes,"
which are another kind of instrument of generalization. The scheme is what there is in common among
several different and analogous actions. For example,
in the case that I was just talking about, once it has
constructed the relationship "pull closer by means of
an intermediary object," it can generalize this to another situation where a different object may be resting on a different support. This is a generalization in
action; it is a scheme.[2] The coordination among
schemes is the equivalence, in a simpler form, of the
coordination of concepts which we do by means of
language. Schemes do not require language because
the scheme is designated by perceptual indices—
"resting upon," "distance," and so forth. There is no
internalized thinking, yet, in the coordination of
schemes. Schemes are instruments of action. But they
are generalizing instruments; we could think of them
as practical concepts. The main difference is that a
concept designates many things at the same time,
whereas a scheme is what is common among different
actions carried out at different times; but a scheme
does tie actions together, just as a concept ties things
together.

EVANS: In discussing the six substages, you point

2 The concept of "scheme" is used in a very broad way to
denote organized patterns of behavior.

out that the child begins with a very, very limited conception of the world and moves gradually to more and more sophisticated conceptions. Toward the end, the child begins to have a concept of itself. Relating object to scheme with respect to the child's self, how could we show this interrelationship? In other words, how can you relate subject and object and the scheme in between?

PIAGET: At the beginning of the sensory-motor period there is no subject. There is a complete lack of differentiation, which Baldwin (1955) called the dualism between the subject and the object. Gradually the subject's actions are differentiated, diversified, and coordinated together. To the extent that they are coordinated, the relationships among objects become specialized, and causal relationships among objects are recognized as being independent of the subject's own actions, and the external world takes on some order. The scheme is the fundamental instrument of this coordination which gives rise to this double-faceted construction of the subject on the one hand and permanent objects on the other. As long as there is no subject, that is, as long as the child does not recognize itself as the origin of its own actions, it also does not recognize the permanency of objects other than itself. At the end of this sensory-motor evolution, there are permanent objects, constituting a universe within which the child's own body exists also. The relationship between the two is progressive coordination.

EVANS: George Herbert Mead (1932), for ex-

ample, sees the individual starting out as "Me"—as
an object to which the mother reacts with phrases
like "You're bad!" "You're good!" and so on. But
eventually the child begins to assert itself. It becomes
an "I." Ultimately there is integration of the "I" and
the "Me" into a "Self." Obviously, Dr. Piaget, you
would not use the same analysis and the same terms
as Mead, would you?

PIAGET: I do not see the analogy, because that is
not there in the beginning; it has to be constructed.
Objects are not there at the beginning either; they,
too, must be constructed. So at the beginning you
have I, which doesn't know itself; and you have objects which are not permanent; and the interactions
between these two poles. Knowledge does not begin
in the I, and it does not begin in the object; it begins
in the interactions. As long as these interactions between subject and object are made up of isolated,
uncoordinated actions, there are neither objects nor
a subject. To the extent that these interactions give
rise to coordinations, then there is a reciprocal and
simultaneous construction of the subject on the one
hand and the object on the other.

EVANS: Could you comment further on your view
of the development of self-awareness?

PIAGET: Baldwin (1955) showed that in the beginning the newborn has no consciousness of itself as
a subject. So it has to construct itself as a subject. For
my part, I was able to show that for a long time it
had no notion of the permanence of objects either.
Tableaux constituted its awareness; these are the
interaction between subject and object but they are

neither a part of the subject nor a part of the object. No differentiation is made between what is self and what is object. The development of the awareness of itself as an acting subject, on the one hand, and a world of objects independent of it, related to one another, causally or spatially, takes place at one and the same time, as the child coordinates its actions more and more. It cannot become aware of itself without at the same time becoming aware of the independence of objects around it, and vice versa. It is the same coordination.

EVANS: As you know, the concept of imitation in early childhood has been of increasing interest to the social learning researchers in American psychology (e.g., Bandura and Walters, 1963). In your view, how does imitation function within the sensory-motor period?

PIAGET: Yes, of course. A scheme in the sense that we were talking about earlier is above all an instrument of assimilation,[3] not of imitation. An object is assimilated into a possible action. But at the same time, the action must be accommodated to the particular characteristics of the object, or of the present situation. Sometimes this accommodation takes precedence over assimilation and becomes an end in itself. To the extent that this happens, we can speak of imitation. There is a very close relationship between the development of imitation and the development

[3] Assimilation involves incorporating a new stimulus event or object into an already existing cognitive framework. Its complement, accommodation, refers to the tendency to adjust one's already existing organization to fit a new stimulus object or event.

of intelligence in general, because imitation depends upon schemes, which of course are sensory-motor intelligence in action. But imitation becomes a separate function to the extent that these actions are carried out in the interests of accommodation for its own sake.

EVANS: The term "circular reaction"[4] obviously is related to this point also. Will you discuss the meaning you ascribe to this phrase?

PIAGET: A circular reaction is a reproductive assimilation. It is the mechanism by which a scheme is developed. The child performs an action, is interested in the result, and repeats the same action again. This repetition is what Baldwin (1955) called a circular reaction. It is this repetition that engenders the scheme.

EVANS: Using the phrase of some of the early association-learning theorists such as E. L. Thorndike (1898) it becomes "stamped in," as it were. Is that right?

PIAGET: No, it is through the circular reaction that it is constructed.

EVANS: If I understand you correctly, then, you are not denying the importance of "stamping in," but you are more interested in the construction of the scheme, which takes place through repetition, and which precedes the stamping in.

---

[4] To elaborate a bit further, the term "circular reaction" as often used in the child development literature refers to repetitive actions of the infant, which occur until the behavior is either extinguished or is strengthened and established ("stamped in") as a result of either internal or external reinforcement.

PIAGET: Yes, quite right. Obviously, there is stamping in. It is so obvious that I don't keep mentioning it. It is a necessary condition, but it is not at all a sufficient condition. In fact, it is entirely insufficient, because in every case there is always construction also.

EVANS: Now, moving from this sensory-motor period, which is a prelanguage stage, you begin the preoperational period at about age two and carry it through to about age seven. Would you care to comment about this period?

PIAGET: The period from two to about seven years of age is characterized by two things. First, the appearance of the semiotic function, that is, the representational, or symbolic, function. This includes language, of course. But not only language. It also includes mental imagery, deferred imitation, drawing —none of which was present before this age. The semiotic function is due to the interiorizing of imitation, and the important aspect here is that the child can now represent to itself an object when it is absent. Now this ability permits the development of a new level of intelligence—intelligence in representation and thought. It is no longer restricted to action. But on this new level, the child must reconstruct everything that it has acquired at the level of actions; it has to reconstruct in conceptual terms everything that it has constructed so far in terms of schemes. This whole period, then, is a preparation for the construction of concrete operations. Since the reconstruction of what has been acquired at the sensory-motor level takes a long time, the concrete operations don't appear immediately as soon as the semiotic function appears. Everything has to be reconstructed again on this level. Furthermore, in the sensory-motor level, actions take place in immediate space and in the present time, while with the appearance of the semiotic function actions can project in the future.

EVANS: Would you care to comment about the preoperational period?

PIAGET: First of all there is the appearance of the semiotic function which is a differentiation of interiorized imitation, and which permits representation and thought.

Secondly, since there is a new plane now—that is, instead of schemes as the only generalizing instruments, there is conceptualization as well—since there is this new plane, everything that has been accomplished on the sensory-motor plane must be reconstructed on this new plane.

Thirdly, on the sensory-motor plane, the child is dealing only with the immediate space around it, and with the present time. Now it has the possibility of representing to itself, and thinking about objects that are far removed in space, or events from the past or future. This, too, supposes a reconstruction. In fact, it requires more than reconstruction; it requires an adaptation to this new, enlarged field. Everything that we have already seen on the sensory-motor plane starts over again now on this representational plane. That is why we do not see operations immediately, and in particular, that is why we do not see con-

servation[5] immediately. Just as the notion of object
permanence takes a long time to be constructed at
the sensory-motor planes, in the same way operational
conservations, or still higher reasoning processes, will
take a long time to be constructed on this new
plane—the more so since its dimensions are much
wider.

EVANS: So in other words, it's really the beginning
of moving from a presymbol level of conceptualization to a level of actual use of symbols?

PIAGET: That's it.

EVANS: Now, from this preoperational level which
you say is until about seven years of age, apparently
you see the organism moving to an operational level
which now becomes increasingly complex. Is this
correct?

PIAGET: Yes, that's right.

EVANS: Could you briefly discuss the mechanisms
in this operational level, which occurs from seven to
eleven years of age?

PIAGET: The essence of an operation at this level
is that it is the interiorization of coordinations which
exist already on the plane of actions, but now since
they are interiorized, there is the possibility of reversibility—one can return to the past in thought. And
furthermore, operations are always coordinated into
total structures, for example, the system of classifica-

---

[5] Conservation refers to a belief that certain attributes of
objects (number, weight, mass) remain invariant in the face of
perceptual transformation. This belief is in accordance with
ordinary experiences the individual has with the physical environment.

tion, or an ordered series, or the series of natural numbers, or one-to-one correspondences, and so forth. Total structures like these constitute a very new field, now, and constitute instruments which are much more powerful than the sensory-motor instruments.

But there is a form of limitation here, in that these instruments apply only to objects themselves. We do not yet have operations which apply to hypotheses, as we will find in an older child. These total structures are still limited by laws such as the one that I call a "grouping"[6]—a structure somewhat resembling a mathematical group, and yet being much more limited than a mathematical group.

EVANS: Of course, the next stage to which you refer is the formal operational period, estimated to appear between the ages of eleven and fifteen. This, of course, is a highly sophisticated level. Could you comment briefly on this period?

PIAGET: The main thing is that we now have the possibility of applying operations not only to objects, but to hypotheses, formulated in words. To work with hypotheses, one must be capable of carrying out operations on operations. The content of any hypothesis is already a form of concrete operations; and then to make some relationship between the hypothesis and the conclusion, this is a new operation. Operations on operations now open up a much

---

[6] A "grouping" is a hybrid logico-algebraic structure, possessing the properties of composition, associativity, identity, and reversibility (Flavell, 1963a). This is primarily a mathematical concept which must be understood within a mathematical context.

broader field of possibilities. In particular, we now have the possibility of the combinatorial, by means of which we can relate any proposition to any other proposition, or any operation to any other operation. In addition, the combinatorial analysis[7] makes it possible to establish sets of subsets which bring together the two types of reversibility which, in concrete operations, always remain separated. These two types of reversibility are negation, on the one hand, and reciprocity on the other. The group of four transformations, as it is called by mathematicians, is one example of a structure in which negation and reciprocity are related to one another. A group such as this is much more powerful still than the grouping of the concrete operational stage.

EVANS: Looking at this entire developmental process, from the sensory-motor all the way through to the higher operational levels, I'm sure that you do not believe that these are fixed. In other words, there is quite a bit of flexibility and individual differences within this developmental model, is there not?

PIAGET: Oh yes, of course, there can be fixations at certain stages; there can be delays and accelerations. But I would even go further. Within the formal operational level, it is entirely possible that some people, for instance those in manual professions, specialized laborers of various sorts, may reach the formal operational level in their particular professional domain, but not right across the board.

[7] Combinatorial analysis refers to a method which guarantees that all possible combinations of variables will be exhaustively inventoried (Flavell, 1963a).

VIEWS OF INTELLIGENCE, VALUES, AND PHILOSOPHY OF RESEARCH

PART III

Overview | In this portion some issues which may be considered controversial by contemporary psychologists as well as some criticisms of Piaget's work are considered. For example, Piaget's view of intelligence as a general concept is discussed as well as Arthur Jensen's controversial position concerning racial differences in I.Q. Piaget reacts to critics of his work who suggest that his method of research produces results that may be a self-filling prophecy. The reader also gains some insight into Piaget, the man, as he discusses the great men he has admired most, misunderstandings of his work, and some of his projects for the future.

EVANS: To move to a different area for a moment, there is a very interesting controversy in the United States involving a report by Dr. Arthur Jensen (1969) of the University of California. This report appears in the *Harvard Educational Review*. Dr. Jensen, looking at what we call the Headstart Program in the United States, suggested that the failure of the Headstart Program might not be due to the fact that the teachers were unable to properly "enrich" the environment of these children who had been in deprived environments. The real problem is that there might have been genetic deficiencies in the black child. He's suggesting that although in one type of intelligence, a fairly concrete type of intelligence, there may be no differences, there may be a type of abstract intelligence in which the Negro child is genetically inferior. I wonder how you feel about this, Dr. Piaget.

PIAGET: I think there are two remarks to be made. First, obviously genetic factors play a role in the development of intelligence. But they can do no more than open certain possibilities. They cannot do anything about actualizing these possibilities. That is, there are no innate structures in the human mind which simply come into being; as I have been pointing out throughout this discussion, all our mental structures must be constructed. So genetic factors or maturational aspects are not adequate for explaining what really takes place at any given stage.

My second comment would be this, how is Jensen measuring intelligence? Is intelligence measured only on the basis of some performance, or are we really getting at the competence, the internal structure? I am afraid that in studies of this sort people have always measured performance, and it is quite obvious that performance will vary according to the social environment. For my part, I have no faith in measures that are based on intelligence quotients or on any other performance measure. So in general, Jensen's conclusion seems to me debatable.

EVANS: I understand that when you were in Paris with the Binet and Simon group who pioneered the measurement of intelligence, you yourself worked on intelligence testing. Was it not during this period that you began to question some of the premises of Binet and Simon in measuring intelligence?

PIAGET: Yes. Of course, when I arrived in Paris as a student, Binet was already dead, but Simon gave me the job of taking Burt's intelligence tests and developing a standardized version in French. As soon as I started on this, what really caught my interest was not a child's answer, but the reasons behind his wrong answers. So as I started looking at the reasons behind children's failure to understand certain things—for example, the inclusion of parts within the whole—I saw that there was a whole series of problems here that were much more interesting than standardizing tests.

EVANS: In other words, qualitative aspects gave body to this whole process.

PIAGET: Yes, that's right. This is not meant to be a criticism of the Binet–Simon tests. They rendered a very great service. But they do pose problems. For example, in the Binet–Simon scale, the seriation of weights is mastered at about ten years of age, while the seriation of lengths is mastered at about seven years of age. Why is there this difference? That's a lovely problem. That's the kind of problem that I wanted to study, rather than just looking at the statistical results.

EVANS: Now, moving to still another area, Dr. Piaget, looking at the general problems that you have dealt with in your work, I think it would be very interesting to hear your own estimate of what you consider your most important contribution. Now I understand that this question is complicated because we could say contributions to philosophy, contributions to mathematics, contributions to psychology, but looking as a whole at your work, which would you consider to be most significant?

PIAGET: Well, I think my role has been above all to raise problems—problems which other people were not seeing, because they were not looking at things from this interdisciplinary point of view. When you look at development from an epistemological perspective, a whole host of problems become very clear, so clear that it seems astonishing that nobody had seen them before. Take the problem of conservations for example. It seems so obvious, that people should have been doing them for generations, but it really took an epistemological point of view to think of doing them.

EVANS: This leads to another point. The whole idea of shifting from a nonempirical philosophical system like epistemology to an empirical psychological system, or using your phrase, genetic epistemology, must present problems. What are the difficulties of moving among disciplines in this way?

PIAGET: That is not an easy question to answer. But I could make the following remarks. All epistemologists, of whatever school, are implicitly calling on psychology. Even if they maintain that they want to avoid any aspect of psychology, that is already a psychological position. The logical positivists, for example, claim to avoid psychology, in maintaining that logic can be reduced to language—to general syntax and semantics. Despite themselves, they have taken a psychological position. What we must keep in mind, then, is that every implicit psychological assumption could be, and should be, verified. This verification is what is missing from epistemology and philosophy. When you get into the field of verification, you are still concerned with the same problems, but they become more precise. Facts help to clarify them.

EVANS: One of the difficulties I believe you have encountered in the transition from the philosophical system to the psychological system has been criticism of your research approach. The "experimental design" traditionally used in psychology involves the stating of a hypothesis and the testing of this hypothesis, which can be done in many ways. Your own research has not often followed this traditional pattern, which makes your approach subject to criticism. How would you answer the critics of your research approach?

PIAGET: I answer this in the simplest way possible. As an experimenter in the field of child development, let us say that you have a preplanned experiment; your hypothesis is formed ahead of time, and the experiment simply tries to answer the question of whether that hypothesis is true or false. Well, in a situation like this, everything is channeled; everything has to fit into a preestablished schema.

But my problem was to find out what the differences are between children and adults, or what differences there are from one stage to the next. If you want to find out what differences there are, you have to go about it in the freest possible, exploratory way. If you start out with a plan, you necessarily falsify everything. Everything that is really interesting to you necessarily must fall outside any plan you have in advance. The reason I don't have experimental plans is that I am looking for new things. For me, an experiment is successful when I find something unexpected, totally unanticipated. That's when things become interesting.

EVANS: Dr. Piaget, would you be satisfied if much of your work were perceived as a generation of significant hypotheses?

PIAGET: Yes, that was the goal.

EVANS: There is clearly a difference between searching for hypotheses and testing hypotheses. It introduces the question of inductive versus deductive research, and this, of course, is not a resolved problem anyway. Is an inductive approach necessarily followed to the exclusion of a deductive approach?

PIAGET: Oh, not always. There is an important relationship between the two. In my work, for instance, I have always tried, often with the help of collaborators, to formalize certain structures. Once we have formalizations, we can make deductions from these structures, and these deductions often give rise to new points of view, and new inductive experiments. There is an interaction between the two.

EVANS: In a recent book which summarizes your work, the American psychologist Phillips (1969) raises a criticism of your approach which I'd be interested to hear your reaction to. He refers to some recent work of Robert Rosenthal (1966) of Harvard University who has argued that a set or expectancy of an experimenter can affect results. He's referring here to a self-fulfilling prophecy. He argues that too much of the research that we have done turns out to be simply finding out what we expect to find out, that we have not controlled for the bias of the experimenter adequately. Dr. Phillips suggested that maybe some of your work or the work of your group could be subject to the same criticism. I think it would be only fair to hear your reaction to Dr. Phillips' comments.

PIAGET: I don't think that is the case. Because as I have just explained in our discussion of induction versus deduction in research, I have a minimum of hypotheses when I start. When the findings are published, of course, by then they have been worked on, and there of course you tie the hypotheses to the facts. But most of the time I began with very incomplete hypotheses, and sometimes they turned out to be wrong, and in simply following the facts I would wind up in a direction quite different from the one I had anticipated.

EVANS: So what you are saying, Dr. Piaget, is that to accuse you of experimenter bias would be incorrect because you don't start out with a bias.

PIAGET: In general, yes.

EVANS: I understand that it depends upon how formal the hypotheses are.

PIAGET: Yes.

EVANS: I noticed before in my question about what you consider your important contributions that you did not touch on your very early work on moral development. As you know, Americans are so concerned about morality, they have particularly paid attention to this work of yours. I was wondering if you might wish to summarize some of the high spots of your findings in the area of moral development.

PIAGET: Gracious, that's ancient history! My work on moral judgment in children was sparked off by the remark of a colleague, who said "that is all very well for facts and evidence, but what goes on when you are dealing with values?" So I tried to study moral judgment in parallel with logical judgment. Well, as usual, in starting without hypotheses, I found unexpected things. For example, the very great difference between the morality of obedience and authority up

to about seven years of age and the morality of cooperation that comes after that, where the idea of
justice starts to develop. And this idea of justice is not
based on adult authority, but is often even at the
expense of adult authority. It is based on relationships
among equals, among the children themselves. All of
that seemed to me rather parallel with the development through the preoperational level[1] and the concrete and formal operational levels[2] in the area of
logical judgment.

EVANS: Now, moving to another, perhaps more
personal, realm, Dr. Piaget, I know that in your very
rich life you have encountered many of the very creative men of our time. I was wondering, among those
men that you have met, whom do you admire most?

PIAGET: Einstein impressed me profoundly, because he took an interest in everything. He asked me
to tell him about our conservation experiments, and
he took a great interest in the fact that this notion of
conservation is so late in developing. He found that
that shed some light for him on the enormous difficulties involved in reaching a level of rational thought.

EVANS: In addition to Einstein, was there another
significant figure with whom you had contact who you
thought was particularly worthwhile?

PIAGET: I remember some conversations with Oppenheimer which were very instructive. They were

[1] The preoperational period is Piaget's second stage of development (two to seven years).
[2] The concrete and formal operational levels are Piaget's last
two developmental periods (seven to fifteen years) and are
characterized by the use of logical relations.

conversations about the role of perception. In the beginning he did not understand what I meant when I said that perception isn't everything, and that it is subordinate to action. But when he came to understand that this subordination had the effect of reinforcing perceptual activities, he changed, he accepted this point of view. These conversations were very instructive, to see a man of that stature thinking about a problem in an area other than his own and to see the phases of his understanding.

EVANS: As you travel around the United States and over the world and meet students and professors, what do you believe to be some of the major misunderstandings of your work?

PIAGET: The major point which has been badly understood is the idea of construction, the idea that structures are new, that they existed neither in the subject nor in the object but have now been built. My friend Berlyne (1965), for instance, has written an article in which he claims that I am a neo-behaviorist, and he bases this on what I say about the nature of physical knowledge of objects and so forth. Then at a symposium in Monterey last year, I heard a lecture by Beilin (1969) who was saying that I am a neo-maturationist, and that if you probe my ideas a bit everything is innate, everything comes from inside. Well, I am neither one nor the other. It comes from inside, of course, but by regulation and construction. This idea of the construction of novelty, this is the idea that is the most difficult to make understood, I think.

EVANS: Have you seen any instances of research

projects that claim to emanate from your ideas that
you think are particularly poor and that you are un-
happy about?

PIAGET: Unhappily, there are many.

EVANS: Could you give us some specific examples,
Dr. Piaget?

PIAGET: No, no, I don't have them in mind right
now. But the main fault with certain of the research
that has been done is that it has broken up my work
and my ideas into little pieces. People go and do a
whole research study on reversibility and pay no
attention at all to any other aspect of the situation. Or
they study conservation, and forget about structures.
In addition to the idea of construction, the other main
idea of mine is that what are constructed are total
structures. The idea that there are total structures
implies that there are interactions among the different
operations of a given level, so if somebody goes and
studies one apart from all the others, naturally, that
gives a mistaken slant to the whole undertaking.

EVANS: Would this mean, therefore, that a lot of
this research that is getting into the journals and is
represented as being derived from your work is going
to lead to even more misunderstanding and more poor
research? In other words, it sounds like a kind of un-
productive circularity is being set up in this manner.

PIAGET: It happens.

EVANS: Dr. Piaget, what are you working on now?
What are your dreams for the future?

PIAGET: Oo la. New projects always follow unfore-
seen problems as they come up. During the past few
years we have been studying causality. It's a point of

view that is very different from the point of view we had had previously. Up to that point, we had always been studying the subject's operations. But in studying causality, we deal instead with objects, and with the resistance that objects present to the subject's understanding. And yet we have found that the development of causality goes through stages which are very comparable to the stages of operational development, except that in this case the operations are attributed to the objects. That is, an object itself is thought to be an operator, and to operate on other objects, and so forth. Now if operations are attributed to objects, this raises the whole problem of the role of one's own actions, and of taking cognizance of one's own actions. How does a child discover in his own actions causal relationships among objects, on the one hand, and the operations of his own thinking, on the other hand? So here is a whole new problem—the relationship between two kinds of abstractions, those based on objects, and those based on actions. We are deep into the problem of these two types of abstractions, and we do not know yet what will come from it. I am now in the midst of studying the data that we have been gathering since October. They are very unexpected indeed, and that will open new directions again. So I have no precise plans for the years to come.

INTERDISCIPLINARY RESEARCH AND RELATING PIAGETIAN CONCEPTS TO EDUCATION

PART IV

Overview | Here Piaget gives his ideas concerning cybernetics, mathematics, and education. He also discusses interdisciplinary research. Finally, he makes some interesting observations concerning Rousseau and Montessori.

EVANS: Dr. Piaget, as I have met some of the individuals from various disciplines who are here on the Institute's staff, I was particularly impressed by Dr. Guy Cellerier[1] who is in the field of cybernetics. How would the models in the field of cybernetics relate to your unique models of human development?

PIAGET: I see a tight relationship between my models and cybernetic models. I have always insisted that the factors traditionally called upon to explain development are inadequate—maturation, experience, social transmission, and so forth. I have always said that another fundamental factor must be added to those, namely, equilibration.[2] Now I did not use cybernetic terminology when I began talking of this factor, but nonetheless since the beginning I have insisted that it was not a

[1] Dr. Cellerier was kind enough to serve as French-English interpreter during the actual dialogue, although the final translation appearing in this volume was completed by Eleanor Duckworth.

[2] Equilibration refers to Piaget's self-regulatory model in which new environmental events are assimilated into existing cognitive structures, and existing structures are transformed to fit new environmental situations.

balance of opposing forces, a simple case of physical equilibrium but that it was a self-regulation. And of course today cybernetics is precisely that, the study of self-regulating models. This self-regulating kernel is at the very heart of all of the development of intelligence. Without it, there is no way of explaining novelty. Knowledge is not predetermined in heredity; it is not predetermined in the things around us—in knowing things around him the subject always adds to them. And if knowledge comes neither ready-made in heredity nor ready-made in the environment, where does novelty come from? I think it must come from self-regulation at each successive level. One can abstract from the coordinations of a given level and build a higher level system from these abstractions; but it is the process of self-regulation which explains the transition from one of these levels to the next higher.

EVANS: As you recall, earlier when we touched on motivation and Freudian theory, we discussed the homeostatic model or the notion of the organism seeking tension reduction or equilibrium. Is this notion of cybernetics to which you just referred so different from this concept?

PIAGET: Oh, I don't think that it differs. I think that it is on a different level. We have homeostasis at every level within biology. Even at the level of the genome, or the very basic genetic units, there is homeostasis; there are physiological homeostases and embryological homeostases. At every level we find homeostasis, so at the level of human conduct, we simply have another self-regulatory system. But homeostasis is not required instantly. It is an arrival point, the result of a process. I translate this arrival point into operational terms—logical, mathematical operations, and so forth. In cybernetics, it is called a perfect regulation, meaning that it is anticipatory, and not just a correction after the action has been carried out a first time. Incidentally, you mention Cellerier. He did a remarkable piece of work on cybernetics and epistemology.

EVANS: The very presence of Dr. Cellerier suggests a unique and important aspect of your Institute, its interdisciplinary nature. Obviously you want to bring together such disciplines as cybernetics, mathematics, biology, philosophy, cultural anthropology, sociology, and psychology to investigate the development of "knowing" in man. In addition to cybernetics, it would be interesting to learn how some of these other disciplines relate to the problems in development of knowing and knowledge. For example, how would cultural anthropology relate to this problem?

PIAGET: Cultural anthropology teaches us two things. First, it can shed light on the generality of the mechanisms that we find. Are these mechanisms specific to our Western societies, or are they universal? So far, the comparisons that people have made seem to show that these mechanisms are common ones, and are to be found in each of the several societies that have been studied from this point of view. With some accelerations or retardations, of course, according to the social mechanisms. So that is the first kind of comparative work, and it is indispensable.

But secondly, what we study here is the ontogenetic

development. We study individuals. Of course, they are individuals within the context of society, but still it is individuals that we focus on. But what cultural anthropology can give us—to the extent that it has a historical dimension, which I realize is difficult— what it can give us is the sociogenesis as well as the psychogenesis. The comparison of the two is indispensable.

EVANS: I noticed a very interesting observation in your Columbia University lecture on "Genetic Epistemology" [included earlier in this volume], another clue concerning the importance you place on an interdisciplinary approach. You stated that you were most fundamentally interested in the matter of how primitive man began to think, how knowledge evolves, and that you became interested in cognitive development in children because this was the only available way of looking at the whole historical development of cognitive processes in man in general. Is this still your fundamental interest?

PIAGET: Yes. Of course, that is quite right. My problem is the development of knowledge in general. Unfortunately, this history is very incomplete—especially at its primitive beginnings, which are actually the most important. So I am doing what biologists do when they cannot constitute a phylogenetic series, they study ontogenesis.

EVANS: Another part of the interdisciplinary team at the Institute is the mathematician. Why do you think that mathematics is so important in the study of the development of knowledge?

PIAGET: Because, along with formal logic, mathematics is the only entirely deductive discipline. Everything in it stems from the subject's activity. It is manmade. What is interesting about physics is the relationship between the subject's activity and reality. What is interesting about mathematics is that it is the totality of what is possible. And of course the totality of what is possible is the subject's own creation. That is, unless one is a Platonist.

EVANS: Now that you have explained why at least some of the various disciplines are relevant to the study of genetic epistemology, the age-old question arises of how so many and varied disciplines can communicate with each other.

PIAGET: During the first year of our Center for Genetic Epistemology, nobody understood anybody else for the first six months. Any problem that one person enunciated was totally incomprehensible to everybody else. So we spent those first six months creating a common language. No, not one common language, but a translation system, and now that we have a translation system, it is all right.

EVANS: Dr. Piaget, perhaps you yourself can relate comfortably to all these disciplines since you would appear to be a generalist in the best sense, with your tremendous background in philosophy, mathematics, biology, and so on. But there are so few generalists of your caliber. How do you think some of your more specialized colleagues can really communicate among themselves in spite of the "translation system" you just mentioned?

PIAGET: First of all, I don't agree that I am truly such a generalist. Above all, what is required is that the head of such an interdisciplinary effort have an encyclopedic ignorance. He has to learn everything, and everybody else can learn by watching how he learns.

EVANS: Moving to another point, Dr. Piaget, do you find much value in applying an analogy between a computer and man's cognitive functioning in a research effort?

PIAGET: It seems that even if we could build a maximally complex computer and keep using it over and over again, this computer will never change. But the human mind with all its complexity continues to actually grow with use. It becomes more complicated.

EVANS: In other words, man's mind will grow whereas computers with continued use will remain static, since the computer is not, to date, self-programming.

PIAGET: Yes. I think that the major difference between a researcher and a computer is that the researcher invents problems. In our work, for instance, each year our main concern is to find a new problem not just to find new solutions.

EVANS: Of course, you are familiar with the work of the prominent Canadian psychologist, Donald Hebb (1949). In reading Professor Hebb's work, we see a possibility for relating his notion of neurophysiological functioning to your work. It seems to me that his theory of progressive organization of the organism, and the brain, would be very close to yours. Do you see some rapprochement between Hebb and yourself?

PIAGET: Yes, certainly, Hebb's view is close to

mine because it has the same idea of progressive organization. He does not think that it is a matter of ready-made Gestalts, nor of associations in the behaviorist's sense. He sees it as a progressive organization.

EVANS: Have you had some personal contact with Professor Hebb?

PIAGET: Occasionally, but unfortunately because of the language problem we have not been able to communicate too effectively.

EVANS: One of the things I find intriguing is the fact that in the United States your work is now coming very rapidly to the attention of people in the field of education, particularly to those involved in education of children in the lower grades. Several recent books have attempted to apply your work to the problems of the teacher. One example is Hans Furth's recent book *Piaget for Teachers* (1970). Is that one direction you would like to see your work go, that is, to be utilized by the teacher as he or she relates to the young student?

PIAGET: Oh, I am convinced that what we have found can be of use in the field of education, in going beyond learning theory, for instance, and suggesting other methods of learning. I think this is basic. But I am not a pedagogue myself, and I don't have any advice to give to educators. All we can do is provide some facts. Still, I think educators can find many new educational methods.

EVANS: Are you concerned about the fact that some people who have not fully comprehended your ideas have moved too quickly into application?

PIAGET: Oh yes. That's the great danger. I have the impression that very few people have understood.

EVANS: There is a kind of a tradition in education that came through in Rousseau's classic work, *Émile* (1762), which is the idea of having the child move into the natural environment, allowing the child to learn by doing and experience. I gather that you would approve of educators applying Rousseau's learn-by-knowing, learn-by-experience notions.

PIAGET: Yes, quite right. Only Rousseau forgot the social aspects. There is only the teacher and Émile.

EVANS: There's more to the world.

PIAGET: Yes, there is a collective Émile.

EVANS: Now, also pursuing the application of your work to education, one of the most interesting movements that we've had in the United States as well as in Europe results from the teachings of the Italian, Maria Montessori. Montessori and some of her followers refer to your work at various points. Have you actually had any personal contact with Montessori?

PIAGET: Yes, I knew Madame Montessori well. I think that Montessori's idea of focusing on activity is excellent, but the materials are disastrous, I think. With a standardized material, one doesn't dare try to change it. And yet the really important thing is for the child to construct his own material.

EVANS: I see. In other words, Montessori has not gone far enough in allowing independence.

PIAGET: Yes, that's it. But no, it's above all the standardized material that is the mistake.

EVANS: What would be your hope with respect to the future influence of your work on the field of education? Would you think the time will come when it will really revolutionize our entire educational system?

PIAGET: Oh, I hope so very much, especially in educating for an experimental frame of mind. For instance, a lot of the mathematics which is being taught now is modern math, but it is often still taught with very archaic methods. And, at least in Europe, nothing at all is done to develop an experimental frame of mind. Experiments are performed in front of the child, but the child is not the experimenter.

EVANS: If I can see the thrust of what you would hope for, Dr. Piaget, concerning education, particularly in the lower grades, it would be a greater opportunity for the child to direct his or her own behavior and experiences, to modify curricula allowing him or her more freedom to develop as an individual at his or her own level. Is this correct?

PIAGET: Yes, but it is important that teachers present children with materials and situations and occasions that allow them to move forward. It is not a matter of just allowing children to do anything. It is a matter of presenting to the children situations which offer new problems, problems that follow on from one another. You need a mixture of direction and freedom.

GENERAL ISSUES IN PSYCHOLOGY

PART V

Overview | In this section, Dr. Piaget responds to the question of the degree to which behavioral scientists should become involved in dealing with current problems. He also relates further experiences with Oppenheimer. Piaget discusses as well the work of Jerome Bruner and Chomsky, and finally gives his views of the relative rationality versus irrationality of man.

EVANS: Dr. Piaget, I would like to move now to a general question that is disturbing many of the behavioral scientists in the United States and, I am sure, all over the world. It seems that society is getting increasingly impatient with the behavioral scientist. It wants him or her to communicate to society and contribute to society now. For example, in the U.S. at the recent American Psychological Association meetings, a group called Psychologists for Social Action banded together. There is pressure for the behavioral scientists to move to help, to do something. Do you feel that the behavioral scientists should attempt to involve themselves in problems of society such as overpopulation, or the means of avoiding war, or poverty, or do you think the scientists should try to stay aloof from these problems lest their objectivity be lost? In other words, can we afford the luxury of sitting back, or should we become involved in problems like poverty, overpopulation, and the insurance of peace?

PIAGET: If a psychologist is involved in activities or some particular research which touches upon possible applications, then I think he has a duty to be concerned with them; but I don't think it is necessary to become involved in social concerns in an artificial way. I do not think that a person should be expected to get involved in a social problem simply because he happens to be a psychologist. He may know nothing in particular about that social problem.

EVANS: Of course, we have had some very tragic situations in the U.S. where the scientist has either developed tremendous guilt feelings about something in which he has succeeded or something in which he has failed in the process of solving a problem for society. The case of J. Robert Oppenheimer is a classic example. You mentioned earlier how you treasured your contact with him at the Princeton Institute for Advanced Study when you were both there together. His experience illustrates how a scientist can be part of a problem-solving effort, developing an atom bomb, and pay for it by lifelong guilt. We had a comparable situation in reverse a few years ago when a U.S. President declared a "war on poverty." Many psychologists or sociologists who became involved in this effort directly became disturbed because in the final analysis they were unable to solve the basic problems. Wouldn't it be better for us as social scientists to simply allow the politicians and bureaucrats to use our findings and not get directly involved in social problem solving?

PIAGET: The problem is much more tragic for physicists. As we discussed earlier, I knew Oppenheimer well and, just as you suggested, I had the impression of a man torn apart over questions like that. For psychologists, I think it is a matter of personal vocation. In spite of the risk of failure, a psychologist who had a sense of social vocation could be more useful than someone who has no particular knowledge of psychology. But above all it seems to me that it would be wrong to impose a duty, in an artificial way, on people who are not particularly competent in the application of their work. I would be very troubled if it were made a moral duty for me to be concerned about the social implications of my work.

EVANS: In other words, it has to be a natural outgrowth of one's temperament or personality, and if it is, fine; but it shouldn't be some kind of artificial commitment.

PIAGET: Yes.

EVANS: Earlier we discussed communication among disciplines here at the Institute. Are you able to communicate with all the various groups and individuals who are working in the fields of psychology and epistemology aside from your group here in Geneva? Or is it even important for you to try to do this?

PIAGET: It is absolutely necessary to keep up to date; but for someone who writes, it is extremely difficult to read. When I first met the Norwegian epistemologist Arne Naess, he said to me, "There seem to be some similarities between what you do and what I do. But I will never read a word of yours, and you will never read a word of mine. We will have to try to find some collaborators who will explain to each of us a little bit about what the other is doing."

EVANS: Have you ever entertained the possibility of holding an international conference to which you might invite people from the various disciplines who have been following your work? Your work has generated a very significant international movement, and as the result of such a movement, a large-scale international conference devoted to your work and its offshoots could be held.

PIAGET: That idea has never occurred to me, and it would terrify me. I prefer individual contacts.

EVANS: Speaking of research in this field by others, it would be interesting to hear what you think of Jerome Bruner's (1966) conceptions. Do you feel that they are compatible with your own?

PIAGET: Bruner's ideas were very near to mine when he wrote his book with Goodnow and Austin (Bruner, Goodnow, Austin, 1952) on the problems of thinking, where they talk in terms of strategies. There we are very close to them, but Bruner is very mobile, you know. He changes a lot. He has new ideas every year. Well, he started working on interpretations, in the area of conservation phenomena, for instance, where he based his work on mental imagery, language, and so forth. Well, for me these seem to be inadequate kinds of explanations.

EVANS: In other words, you feel that Bruner's (1966) work has gone through a kind of evolution from a stage at which he was operating more clearly in the area of the development of knowledge in the sense that you have, to the present time where he has been moving into the area of language, and may even be too involved with linguistics.

PIAGET: Oh, I think it is quite legitimate to go outside psychology and make use of linguistics. Only I wish he would allow me the same right to go outside psychology and make use of logic. Linguistics seems to him perfectly natural, but logic seems to frighten him. For my part, I think we need to look at both.

EVANS: In other words, are you stating that perhaps Bruner is not being eclectic enough?

PIAGET: No, it is not that. It's that he is reticent about logic. He thinks it belongs to philosophy, not to science. But, above all, he doesn't believe in operations. He uses them every day, but he doesn't believe in them.

EVANS: Perhaps one reason for Bruner's emphasis is that the problem of language in general is extremely important to the American psychologist. For example, B. F. Skinner has had a great deal of difficulty in his work in dealing with experience or cognitive processes. But in his book *Verbal Behavior* (Skinner, 1968) he is more or less willing to admit language into the system because he can categorize language as a response. Now if I understand you correctly, Dr. Piaget, you are saying that once a psychologist begins to become too involved with language, it begins to bind him to this area and he ignores others.

PIAGET: Yes, certainly. At every level we have to keep in mind the relationship between language and thinking. Here in Geneva we are fortunate in having

an excellent linguist and psycholinguist, Madame Sinclair. She was able to show a close relationship between the development of operations and the development of language. The most interesting thing was that
she showed that development in language does not
carry along with it a corresponding development in
operations, while the reverse does turn out to be true.

EVANS: That, of course, was a classic finding. This
was something that you had postulated much earlier
and here Dr. Sinclair has verified it. Isn't this correct?

PIAGET: Oh yes, it was an important verification.
But also I think that the current tendencies in linguistics, since Chomsky, are much closer to what I thought
than the tendencies were at the time of Bloomfield,
or purely sensory linguistics.

EVANS: You mention Dr. Chomsky (1968). His
functional linguistics theory represents the point of
view that not only would be closer to yours, Dr.
Piaget, but would be in firm opposition to Dr.
Skinner. In fact, are you aware of this controversy
between Skinner and Chomsky?

PIAGET: Yes, of course. I think Chomsky is on the
right side by a wide margin.

EVANS: Moving to another area, Dr. Piaget, one
of the biggest single issues American psychology students cope with is the question of whether the human
organism is rational or irrational. Now if we read
Freudian theory, we seem to observe the human
organism as primarily irrational with relatively little
capability for rationality. If we look at your work, we
seem to see a human organism who is nearly totally

rational with perhaps only a bit of irrationality. Is this a correct comparison?

PIAGET: It is unkind to Freud. But I think that neither Freud nor I should be taken as the authority in this matter, but rather the biologists. Cannon (e.g., 1934) and others, for instance, with their notion of homeostasis which we discussed in other contexts earlier, show that there is a wisdom of the body.

LEARNING, CURIOSITY, AND CREATIVITY

PART VI

Overview | In this part of the dialogue, Piaget discusses learning, reinforcers, the child as an "experimenter," and the curiosity of the child. Piaget and I also discuss Piaget's earlier work, universal behavior versus cultural relativism, and finally creativity.

EVANS: As we discussed earlier, Dr. Piaget, in American psychology we find learning and learning theory of great interest to us, particularly in learning as a function of external reinforcement as Skinner has emphasized. Now, it's very clear, Dr. Piaget, as you mentioned earlier, that you do not focus on learning as obviously as many American psychologists do, but does that necessarily suggest that you feel that learning is not important, or is it a question of your system redefining learning?

PIAGET: We have to redefine learning. We have to think of it differently. First of all, learning depends upon the stage of development, or on the competence, as the embryologists put it. And development is not simply the sum total of what the individual has learned.

Secondly, in thinking of reinforcements, we must think not only of external reinforcements but of internal reinforcements, through self-regulation.

I think there has to be a new approach in learning research, and that is just what Barbel Inhelder and Madame Sinclair and Magali Bovet are working on now. They are looking for the learning processes which are based on the developmental factors that our psychogenetic studies have revealed.

EVANS: A fascinating aspect of your approach is that you appear to view the psychologist-genetic epistemologist as an experimenter who in turn views the child also as an experimenter, and one experimenter (the psychologist) arranges the opportunities for the other experimenter (the child) to carry on his or her experiments. Wouldn't that be one simple way of looking at a lot of your work?

PIAGET: That's right.

EVANS: So if we were to look around your laboratory and see some of your students and watch what they're doing, we would observe (as I, indeed, have) a great respect for this natural experimental potential of the child and see the students arranging for an opportunity to observe this experimental behavior. So you are really training your students to respect the child as a natural experimenter.

PIAGET: That's right.

EVANS: A parallel for this child-experimenter notion can be found in earlier psychological literature. The term "curiosity" was generally discussed as a pervasive motive. Would you say that this natural curiosity is in fact the important thing in the process of human development?

PIAGET: Yes, yes. But it is a curiosity which goes through various steps, in the sense that whenever one problem is solved, new problems are opened up. These are new avenues for curiosity. We have to follow this development of problems. We should not allow children a completely free rein on the one hand, nor channel them too narrowly on the other hand.

EVANS: Well, to draw the parallel here, Freud may see the organism born an animal, seeking primarily to satisfy biological, often unconscious needs. You also see the organism as seeking primarily to satisfy a need, but in focusing on curiosity you are dealing with a seemingly more rational need.

PIAGET: Yes, but I think that there is a transition between biological satisfaction and intellectual satisfaction. As sense organs and motoricity widen an organism's field of activity, then biological needs take on an aspect of implicit curiosity which keeps growing and flourishing. We see it already in primates, for example. Chimpanzees demonstrate intellectual curiosity.

For example, once when one of my children was in his playpen—this was when he was at the sensory-motor level, well before any language—I held out an object to him horizontally, so that if he simply tried to pull it towards himself, it was blocked by the rails of the playpen. He tried various positions, and finally got it in, but he got it in by chance, and he wasn't satisfied. He put it back outside the playpen and tried to do it again, and continued until he understood how he had to turn it to get it through the rails. He wasn't satisfied just to succeed. He wasn't satisfied until he understood how it worked.

EVANS: Isn't this a very important part of this whole theory—the fact that the child in a sense is intrigued by the operation as much as the end product of all this? The child wants to study this operational process; it is not satisfied with simply the end result.

PIAGET: Yes. Yes. But at a certain level.

EVANS: Another question that I think is really quite fascinating as we look at your work, Dr. Piaget, is the question of how did you yourself begin to work with the child? Now, of course, you mentioned a moment ago that you observed your own children. But thinking back to your very earliest beginnings working with children and trying to start to develop some of these ideas, how did you go about it? Obviously the methodology developed over time; it wasn't there immediately; it must have taken quite a bit of time for you to develop it. Looking back at the very beginning of your experiences, what were some of the things that you did wrong when you first started working with children?

PIAGET: Oh, my errors. I believed in language too much. I had the children talk instead of experiment.

EVANS: This is a very important thing. In other words, almost from the very beginning you began to see the limitations of overemphasizing language in this work.

PIAGET: Not right at the beginning, I wasn't sensitive to that. It wasn't until I had my own children and saw what they did before language.

EVANS: Going back to your very beginning activity, it is clear that coming out of your background as an epistemologist and as one with a tremendous background in biology and mathematics, when you suddenly ran over and started working with children,

live children, you were no longer sitting in an armchair; you were no longer working with animals or
theorems, you were beginning to do things with
children. How did your colleagues react to you?
Didn't they think that this was a rather strange way
for an armchair philosopher or laboratory scientist to
start behaving?

PIAGET: My colleagues were disturbed. An old
botanist friend of mine said, "You, you are lost to
science." But then he had me tell him what I was
doing, and he became all excited, and said, "Oh, if
I were only a psychologist . . . !"

EVANS: Now were you in your early work ever
discouraged? In other words, here you were moving
into a revolutionarily new subject; you were taking
problems in epistemology that have always been considered in an armchair, and you were trying to subject them to some empirical tests. Did you almost
immediately begin to see that this was leading to
something very worthwhile or were you sometimes
discouraged at the beginning?

PIAGET: Oh no, never.

EVANS: Moving now to another area, I think that
one of the problems in psychology in general is the
question of universal patterns in the individual versus
patterns that are culturally developed. Now as I see
your developmental stages, you're talking about universals, things that are characteristic of the cognitive
structures of all human organisms, and you would
probably say, in effect, that you could go to every
single culture and you would find these same universals.

PIAGET: Oh yes.

EVANS: So, in a sense when we talk about cultural relativism, the effect that culture can have in shaping properties of an individual, it's not that you would be opposed to the idea of cultural relativism, but you would say that cultures have their impact within the universal framework of development.

PIAGET: I would be inclined to believe that, yes. Like Durkheim (1953), I believe that underlying "societies" there is "Society"; that is, certain common mechanisms of interchange, of cooperation, that can be found in all societies.

EVANS: And so, what you're really saying is that all societies have certain unique characteristics and all individuals in their cognitive development have universal characteristics. So that all you really have, as far as the effects of a given culture on the individual are concerned, are a finite number of permutations and combinations.

PIAGET: I don't know if the number is finite; I think there is every transition between the common kernel and the variations. But at least there is a common kernel.

EVANS: Supposing we were to observe a three-year-old child in a preliterate society in the Congo who is physically and intellectually normal. For comparison purposes, supposing we were to observe a three-year-old child here in Geneva, also physically and intellectually normal. Now the three-year-old from the preliterate society has had much less verbal language stimulation than the child raised here in Geneva who would have had tremendous exposure to language at the very beginning. What would be some of the differences that you would expect to find between these two children?

PIAGET: I would expect to find a difference of speed, according to the conditions. The order of the stages would be the same, but the speed would be different. There would be some accelerations.

EVANS: In other words, you are saying that the culture could have the effect of decelerating or accelerating stages. Is this correct?

PIAGET: Yes, at the very least. But it can diversify, too, of course.

EVANS: Now to pursue this idea for a moment, suppose we could stimulate the progress of the cognitive stages maximally to achieve an ideal development process, would this be a means of developing highly creative individuals? In other words, we don't know very much about creativity. Could we intervene into the system of cognitive development with some of the insights from your research as a means of increasing the probability that we will produce a highly creative individual?

PIAGET: Oh, I think so. Oh, I think so.

EVANS: In this sense, what would you define as a creative individual?

PIAGET: It is to build a structure that is not preformed, neither in hereditary nor in social environment, nor in the physical environment.

EVANS: Now in the 1920s a certain epistemologist by the name of Piaget suddenly started to study children. Would that be considered creative?

PIAGET: No. It is just an opening of possibilities or new combinations.

EVANS: Well, are not new combinations creative?

PIAGET: Oh, if they are contained in the possibilities of what came immediately before, that's not creative.

EVANS: On this, I must take issue with you, Dr. Piaget. I believe your work is not only creative but it is a generative creativity judging by the amount of new research you have stimulated. Finally, Dr. Piaget, I was wondering what is your reaction to the fact that you're sort of caught between two disciplines. On the one hand, the philosophers and epistemologists don't really understand the direction of your work and on the other hand, many psychologists have great difficulty fully understanding your work. What do you do in a situation like this?

PIAGET: I wait.

PIAGET'S DEVELOPMENTAL MODEL AND COMPARISONS WITH SKINNER, FREUD, AND ERIKSON

BY RICHARD I. EVANS, WILLIAM J. KROSSNER, AND HARVEY J. GINSBURG

PART VII

Overview | Here we develop in more detail Piaget's model of intellectual development and try in the process to define some of the key words and phrases Piaget uses so that the reader is provided with a small glossary. We also briefly compare Piaget's views with those of Skinner, Freud, and Erikson.

As would be expected, due to the comprehensive nature of Piaget's theoretical approach, a thoroughgoing examination of his conceptual organization of the development of thought and knowledge was admittedly beyond the scope of the Evans-Piaget dialogue. The discussion by Elkind in the beginning of this volume as well as Piaget's intriguing autobiography and his article tracing the development of "genetic epistemology" provide relevant background for the dialogue. However, "fleshing out" some aspects of Piaget's ideas as they have been more specifically presented in the dialogue may also be of value to the reader. So this section has a threefold purpose: (1) to provide a general outline of Piaget's theory of intellectual development; (2) within the context of this outline to provide the reader with a basic glossary that will serve to clarify further some of the more technical terminology in the dialogue; (3) since B. F. Skinner, Sigmund Freud, and Erik Erikson are mentioned in the dialogue, to provide a brief comparison of Piaget's views with their views. This is offered the reader so that he can become familiar with at least a few of the similarities and contrasts among these notable contributors to contemporary psychology. The reader may also wish to examine the earlier books in this series which dealt with other notable psychologists. In this way, he may gain a basis for further comparisons (Evans, 1964, 1966, 1968, 1969a, 1969c, 1971) by examining responses to questions similar to those asked Piaget in this book.

As is evident in the dialogue, Piaget's concept of intelligence is an important beginning of Piaget's work. It was his reservations concerning early efforts to study intelligence that really led him to formulate many of his original ideas.

Intellectual growth has been broadly defined by Piaget in terms of a biological adaptation model. Intelligence is viewed as an open system which extends into the environment to obtain knowledge, but which also tends to close in terms of mental structure to encompass already extant organizational features. It is thus an evolutionary advance that oscillates between opening (transforming existent structures in response to the environment) and closing (incorporating attributes of the environment into existing structures), so that a homeostatic balance is achieved (Nash, 1970). Piaget has termed this balance *equilibration*. It is through the complementary processes of assimilation and accommodation that this state of equilibrium is achieved. *Assimilation* involves the incorporation of new events into preexisting cognitive structures. *Accommodation* involves the transformation of an already existing structure in response to the environment. Intellectual growth is thus seen as the resolution of tension between assimilation and accommodation. It is an active, organized process of assimilating the new to the old and accommodating the old to the new (Flavell, 1963).

Once a dynamic balance has been struck between accommodation and assimilation, it persists for a time and is called a stage of intellectual development. A stage is succeeded only by a subsequent stage that is still more successful in permitting intellectual functioning and mastery of the environment.

As his experimental technique, Piaget employs a special interview or clinical method for studying the development of intellectual capacity. Questions are posed with respect to concrete materials shown to the child, which are manipulated either by the experimenter or the child. Questions pertaining to problems arising from such a manipulation of the materials are stated in a flexible and unstandardized manner. From the manipulations and answers, the experimenter can infer the cognitive operations the child is employing. Piaget employs this method, usually with simple materials such as beakers of water, but handled in an ingenious way, to determine cognitive capacities and processes of children during particular stages.

Piaget's Developmental Model

As indicated by Piaget in the dialogue, his developmental model consists of four major periods of intellectual development.

I. Sensory-Motor Period (birth to two years)

During the sensory-motor period, the infant moves from a neonatal, reflexive level marked by a complete lack of self-world differentiation (the child does not distinguish between himself and the rest of the world) to a relatively coherent organization capable of sensory-motor actions within its immediate environment. The organization is a practical one and involves simple perceptual and motor adjustments to environmental phenomena rather than symbolic manipulations of them. Piaget describes six major substages of this period. The stages reflect subtly evolving organizational transitions for these simple motor and perceptual adjustments, until by the end of the sensory-motor period, a rudimentary ability to symbolize actions or events internally is achieved.

The first stage, that of *reflexes* (birth to one month), involves the increased efficiency with which innate reflexes come to function. It is important to note that one of Piaget's primary considerations of reflexive behavior at this stage is that even these basic types of adaptations are not merely evoked by direct external stimulation; rather, the infant (as an active rather than passive creature) often initiates reflexive activity itself.

During the second stage of sensory-motor development (one to four months), *primary circular reactions*
occur. These are nonintentional spontaneous actions
that center about the infant's body (hence they are
termed primary) and that are repeated over and over
(circular) until the adaptation becomes strengthened
and established. Thus, behavior in the second stage is
characterized by the appearance of the repetition of
simple acts. Such actions are nonpurposeful and are
repeated for their own sake. Examples of primary circular reactions would be repetitive thumb-sucking, or
the repeated action of fingering a blanket.

The remaining four stages of the sensory-motor
period are marked by an ever increasing intentionality
on the part of the child. Of importance in stage three
(four to eight months) is the development of *secondary circular reactions*. During this stage the infant's awareness of the external environment expands.
Infant reactions during this stage, rather than focusing primarily on bodily actions, now involve the
infant's manipulation of events or objects in the external environment. Hence, such reactions are termed
secondary. Activity during this stage is also characterized by circularity (actions are repeated over and
over). However, reactions in this third stage are not
merely repeated for their own sake but are repeated
because of the interesting stimulus effect created by
particular activity. Interesting results are maintained
by repeating those actions (discovered by chance)
that initially led to the production of the novel alteration of the external object or event. An example of a
secondary circular reaction would be an infant who

repeatedly waves its arms in order to produce movement in a toy suspended above its crib.

The fourth sensory-motor stage (eight to twelve months) involves the coordination of *secondary reactions*. Means-ends are clearly differentiated; for the first time the infant's behavior is truly intentional in nature and the child begins to solve simple problems. Previously unassociated *schemes* (a scheme is a general response used to solve a particular problem) of action are associated in a novel manner. The infant applies one scheme as a means to achieve a goal; another familiar scheme is employed to treat the goal once it is achieved. This novel coordination of secondary reactions is made possible by the infant's ability to generalize or transfer the scheme used as a means from the situation in which it was originally utilized.

During stage four, self and world become progressively differentiated. *Object permanence* is established. If the infant watches an object being hidden from view, it comes to know that this object still has an objective existence even though it is detached from the infant's own actions. The following example should serve to clarify the marked intentionality and the concept of object permanence that characterize the fourth sensory-motor stage. Suppose the infant views a favorite toy, which is slowly covered by a cloth. After the object is completely hidden, Piaget maintains that an infant in stage three of sensory-motor development no longer acknowledges the objective existence of the object; for this child, it is "out of sight, out of mind." Given this simple situation, an infant in stage four is quite able to comprehend the independent existence of the toy. Both infants may come to pull the cloth off the object. The stage three infant does so, perhaps merely to watch the movement of the cloth (the movement being an interesting stimulus event in and of itself). After the cloth is pulled away from the toy, the stage three infant may even accidentally discover the "re-existence" of the object and employ the secondary reaction of reaching to gain access to the toy. In contrast, the infant in stage four of the sensory-motor period clearly has the toy in mind from the beginning and does not stumble upon it accidentally. The cloth that covers the object is perceived as an obstacle that does not allow direct attainment of the goal. The pulling of the cloth is employed as a means of obtaining the desired goal; thus, unlike the activity in stage three, the movement of the cloth is not an end in itself. The action of pulling the cloth serves as a means to an end that is related to and coordinated with the end action of reaching for the toy. This ability to uniquely combine previously unconnected schemes of action (using one scheme as a means for attaining the goal and a second scheme for dealing with the goal) in a means-end relationship forms the basis of simple problem-solving activity on the part of the infant.

The concept of object permanence is not fully articulated by stage four. The infant in the fourth stage has considerable difficulty if the movements of an object are somewhat complex or if the object is spatially displaced from the area where it was initially hidden. For example, if a toy is repeatedly hidden under a pillow the stage four infant will search for it. But if the object is then hidden under a second pillow, the infant will continue to search under the first pillow, even though he clearly observed the toy being hidden under the second pillow. It is as if an attribute of the object is the place or position that was associated with previously successful attempts to uncover the object hidden from view. During the fifth stage of the sensory-motor period (twelve to eighteen months), the infant becomes aware of the fact that an object can be spatially displaced and still retain a permanence of its own. The constancy of an object is thus better established; permanence is now something apart from the infant's past success in finding the object in one particular place. Another aspect of stage five is the development of *tertiary circular reactions*. These reactions are defined in terms of more effective and advanced methods of exploring new objects or environmental events by means of novel experimentation. The interest in novelty for its own sake is the primary attribute of a tertiary circular reaction. Through active trial-and-error experimentation the infant discovers new means for attaining a goal. Whereas in stage four, the behavior leading to a goal was rather stereotyped, the stage five infant actively seeks and experiments with novel means of attaining a particular end. It does not solely rely on activities that proved to be previously successful. Rather than moving a pillow with his hand to obtain a hidden toy, the infant approaches the problem in many ways. It may attempt to kick the pillow with its feet or use a stick to displace the pillow. The child in the fifth stage does not initiate action merely in order to obtain the desired goal; action is initiated so that means-end relationships can be fully explored. The infant is interested in novel variation and how that variation affects the object or his ability to obtain the object.

Stage six (eighteen to twenty-four months) is characterized by the transition from overt action to covert mental representation. The child is capable of utilizing mental symbols to refer to objects absent from the immediate environment. The constraint of immediate experience as a requisite for purposeful activity is lessened. During this stage the child is able to *defer imitation*, to reproduce from memory the behavior of an absent model. The child is capable of representing the absent model through some symbolic form. The infant in this final stage of sensory-motor development is capable of *internal experimentation*, an internalized mental exploration of relationships between ways and means. In other words, with the advent of mental representation and invention, the child is able to symbolize actions or events before actually acting out any particular behavior. Solutions to problems are considered in terms of a mental rather than a physical dimension. During this last stage of the sensory-motor period the concept of object permanence is more clearly established. The child now will search for a spatially displaced object where it last disappeared from view, rather than in the area where it was last hidden. This indicates that the child recognizes the fact that an object can be displaced and still maintain external objectivity.

II. Preoperational Period (two to seven years)

The *preconceptual stage* (from two to four years of age) is the first of the two subdivisions of the pre-operational period. Evolving from the last stage of the sensory-motor period, the genesis of conceptual thought occurs in the preconceptual stage. During this stage the child develops linguistic skills and the ability to construct symbols; it begins to distinguish between *signifiers* (words and images that stand for objective events or objects) and *significates* (perceptually absent events to which those words or images refer). The child is able to differentiate "daddy putting on his coat" (signifier) and the concept that "daddy putting on his coat" refers to the as yet perceptually absent event of daddy going away (the significate). The appearance of *symbolic function* (employing a mental image, symbol, word, or an object to stand for or represent an event that is not immediately present) frees the child from acting only on considerations that are physically apparent in the immediate environment. Symbolic function allows the child to apply past experience to present events.

Another basic feature of this stage is that imitation becomes less overt and is increasingly internalized. Imagination during play becomes apparent; the child develops the ability to treat objects as symbols of things other than themselves (it may employ a broom for an imagined horse or use a tin can as a telephone receiver). During this stage the child increasingly begins to experience mental representations of the external world and of its own actions.

However, many characteristics of thought in the preconceptual stage differ markedly from later, mature thought processes. For example, children at this level cannot formulate a set of rules that allows an object to be included within a specific set of objects. Piaget defines *syncretism* as the tendency to group unrelated events or items together into a very confused whole. For example, rather than employing some rule of class membership (the set of all objects employed as cooking utensils) to define what items belong in the kitchen, children in the preconceptual period do not attempt to determine particular attributes that are common to a set of objects. Instead, many unrelated items are classified together (cookies, a woman, a wall clock, matches, etc., are grouped together and labeled "kitchen"). Preconceptual thought is also *egocentric;* the child thinks only in terms of its own point of view and does not possess the ability to take the role of another individual. It is also unable to critically evaluate its own thoughts (e.g., the child neither thinks about its own thinking nor attempts to consider any possible contradictions in its thought processes).

Thought during the preconceptual stage also tends to be *centered;* the child focuses upon one particular aspect or dimension of a stimulus array at a time. Multiple dimensions of a problem are never considered simultaneously. While one particular aspect of an event is centered upon, other relevant dimensions are overlooked and neglected. Singular features are not combined into a multidimensional, integrated pattern.

The *intuitive stage* is the second of the two pre-operational subdivisions lasting from approximately four to seven years of age. It is a preparation period for the stage of concrete operations. During this stage, more complex thoughts and images are constructed than in the preceding stage, and the child progressively develops its ability to conceptualize. A rudimentary concept of class and class inclusion is established, but is based on perceptual similarity instead of logical or relational considerations. For example, rather than classifying a starfish in terms of phyletic comparison, it may be classed as a type of rock or stone due to its perceptual similarity with such objects. Thus, thought at this stage is still largely restricted to the child's experiential perceptual milieu. Its comprehension of events is still largely dominated by an inability to perceive more than one salient dimension of a situation at a time.

Another critical aspect of thought, which lasts throughout the preoperational period, is its *irreversibility*. Irreversible thought is defined as the inability to consider a series of reverse operations that will restore an original situation.

Piaget's classic experiments, which demonstrate the inability of the preoperational child to acknowledge the phenomenon of *conservation* (that quantities of liquid and mass, or number of objects in an array, remain invariant in the face of perceptual transformations), serve to characterize many of the dominant thought processes of children during this entire period. Certain qualities of preoperational thought make it impossible for a child at this level to recognize that a quantity of water remains constant (is conserved) in spite of differences in the form of the container into which the water is poured. If water is poured into two identical glasses up to the same level, the child will readily acknowledge that both glasses have the same amount of water. If the water in one glass is then poured into a taller, narrower container (so that the level of water is higher in the new container), the preoperational child will insist that the taller, narrower glass contains more water. It may be that a child in the preconceptual stage of the preoperational period fails to conserve because it attends to only one salient aspect of the problem (the height of the liquid in the columns of water) while neglecting equally important aspects of the problem; namely, that the second container differs in width as well as height from the comparison glass. By perceptually centering on only one dimension at a time, the child is incapable of simultaneously coordinating two or more dimensional attributes of the problem.

It may be that children in the second (intuitive) stage of the preoperational period fail to conserve because their ability to define abstract concepts like quantity or amount is also restricted by perceptual attributes of the problem. This child might intuitively equate "height" with its concept of quantity ("more"). Thus, the level of the liquid in the two containers again determines the child's concept of quantity. In either case, thought is marked by its irreversibility. The preoperational child is unaware that an operation exists that will restore the original situation. This child is not cognizant of the fact that if the water in the taller, narrower glass is poured back into the first of the identical containers it would again assume its original height.

Of course, these unique thought processes like centration and irreversibility are highly interrelated. For example, a child in the preoperational period may see that when the water is poured back into the original container (reverse operation) it again assumes a height equal to that of the other identical container. The child may then acknowledge that the amount of water in the two glasses is equal, yet, when a transformation occurs again (i.e., when the water is poured into the tall, narrow glass), for one reason or another, the preoperational child loses sight of this reverse operation, does not consider it, and continues to rely on salient perceptual characteristics of the stimulus array.

III. Concrete Operational Period (seven to eleven years)

Since birth, the dominant mental activities have changed from overt actions (in the sensory-motor period) to perceptions (in the preoperational period) to intellectual operations (in the period of concrete operations). Those operations occur within the framework of what Piaget calls *mobility* of thinking: the ability to deploy reversibility, to de-center, to be able to take the viewpoint of another and to conceptualize class relations. During the concrete operational period the child establishes foundations for the type of logical thinking that is identified with the next and final period of intellectual development.

There are many differences between the child in the preceding period and the child in the period of concrete operations. Given the same conservation problem as the preoperational child, children in the concrete operational period comprehend the idea that quantity remains invariant despite perceptual transformations. The thinking of the child at this stage is characterized by the deployment of reverse operations. Thus the child now may correctly answer questions about conservation of liquid by stating, "The amount of water (after the transformation) is still the same, because you can pour the water from the tall, narrow glass back into the original container, and the level of water in the two identical glasses will still be the same."

Another difference between preoperational and concrete operational thinking is that the child in the period of concrete operations has developed a clearly defined concept of class and class inclusion. The development of the ability to think simultaneously about part-whole relationships is one component of this newly established capability. For example, if preoperational children are shown eight yellow and four brown pieces of candy, and are asked, "Are there more yellow candies or more candies?," they are likely to reply, "More yellow candies." Children at the level of concrete operations, however, are likely initially to respond with puzzlement to the seemingly absurd nature of the question. They will eventually answer by saying, "There are more candies (total) than yellow candies." Their answer to this question indicates a clear differentiation between parts and wholes, an ability to reason simultaneously about part-whole relationships and a knowledge that elemental subclasses (brown and yellow pieces of candy) can be included within broader class categories (candies, in general).

Other major differences between preoperational and concrete operational thought include:

1) The ability to utilize *relational terms*. The preoperational child regards relational expressions such as "darker" or "larger" in terms of absolute attributes of objects as opposed to relative attributes between objects. Darker means very dark instead of darker than another object; larger means very large as contrasted with the relative concept of larger than a second or third object. The child in the period of concrete operations can view objects or events in a relative fashion. Given the problem, "If A is smaller than B and B is smaller than C, is A smaller than C?," the concrete operational child has the capacity to solve the problem by considering the relative relationships between each of the material objects.

2) The child in this period possesses the ability to arrange objects in terms of some quantitative dimension, such as weight, size, or ordinal scale. Piaget terms this conceptual ability *seriation*. Seriation is critical for understanding the relationship one number has to another and is a necessary requisite for preliminary mathematical thought.

3) The child in the period of concrete operations is also able to utilize a mental representation of a series

of actions. The child in the preceding stage may be able to walk a short distance to school by knowing precise places where it is to turn right or left, but has no concept of the overall route it travels when it goes to school. The concrete operational child is quite able to map out the entire series of actions it took while walking to school; it is able to conceptualize the route beforehand.

Concrete operations are structured and organized in terms of truly concrete phenomena—events that generally occur in the immediate present. Consideration of potentiality (the manner in which events may possibly occur) or reference to future events or situations is rather limited in scope. It is this concrete approach to reality that differentiates the period of concrete operations from the final period of intellectual development.

IV. Formal Operational Period (eleven to fifteen years)

This period covers the ages from eleven to fifteen years. The most general attribute of formal operational thinking is the realization that reality is but one of a set of all possibilities. The adolescent's reasoning is *hypothetico-deductive;* it begins with a consideration of a given problem in terms of a conceptualization of all possible relations that could hold true (a set of possible hypotheses), and then, through a process of experimentation combined with logical analysis, each individual hypothesis is either confirmed or rejected. The ability to generate all possible solution hypotheses and then check the validity of each through a logical analysis is the hallmark of the period of formal operations.

Thinking at this level is above all *propositional*. The adolescent manipulates the raw data he encounters into organized statements or propositions and then develops logical connections between them. Also, formal operational thinking is interpropositional; that is, it involves the logical relations among the propositions formed from the raw data. Piaget refers to these operations as *second-order operations*, or operations on operations.

The individual at the level of formal operational thought is able to employ a *combinatorial analysis* to solve a specific problem. Suppose one is given four buckets of paint, each consisting of a different primary color. The problem is to combine two of the four in order to create a unique color. The individual in the period of formal operations realizes that it must combine one with two, one with three, one with four, two with three, etc. All possible combinations are considered. Given this same problem the child during the period of concrete operations could not consider all possibilities, only those possibilities related to the tangible present. Hence, this child would only consider, for example, the combinations of buckets one and two, two and three, and three and four.

The adolescent also has the capacity to apply *simplifying rules* as a higher-order operation to arrive at the solution of a problem. For example, suppose the individual is given a tub of water and a large variety of different objects, and is called upon to select only those objects that will float. The individual in the period of formal operations is no longer tied to the concrete; it does not have to put each object into the water to determine whether or not it will float. Instead, this individual applies a simplifying rule. It knows that wooden objects float; it may then experimentally determine which objects arrayed before him are made of wood by employing some empirical test. The necessity of directly placing each of the objects into the water is thus eliminated. The capacity to employ combinatorial analyses and simplifying rules forms the basic groundwork of algebraic thought and is an absolute prerequisite for the comprehension of higher mathematical reasoning.

The domination of reality by possibility also characterizes the individual's relationship with the future. Thought about future events becomes well articulated. The remote or distant event can be viewed in terms of a set of hypothetical possibilities; the individual's thought processes no longer need be restricted to the present or near present. Serious consideration of future events is achieved only during the period of formal operations.

One final characteristic of formal operational thought is summarized by the following often-quoted type of adolescent remark: "I found myself thinking about my future and then I began to think about why I was thinking about my future, and then I began to think about why I was thinking about why I was thinking about my future." Preoccupation with the mechanisms of thought appears to be a primary feature of cognitive functioning during the period of formal operations.

Finally, in terms of social interaction, which is, as will be indicated later, not emphasized as such by Piaget, it would appear that Piaget is suggesting that motivation and evaluation come to depend on ideals and events, which tend to be judged on the basis of approximations of the theoretical state of affairs that fulfills these ideals. The adolescent views its own plans and activities as they relate to an idealized social group. The individual begins to think of itself as a full-fledged member of society.

Comparisons with Skinner, Freud, and Erikson

In conclusion, it might be interesting to introduce briefly at least some of the differences between Piaget and Skinner, Freud, and Erikson. First to compare Piaget and Skinner: Piaget appears to view the child as an active participant in the developmental process; in contrast, Skinner appears to view the child more as shaped by environmental contingencies of reinforcement. In other words, Skinner emphasizes the reactive aspects of the child's behavior as opposed to its active seeking and directing of responses. In line with this, Piaget seems to consider the principles of behavior theory to be too mechanical with a resultant over-emphasis on habit development. Thus, Skinner would see no need for such concepts as awareness, intention, and comprehension; Piaget, in contrast, prefers these mentalistic concepts. Piaget is a stage theorist: to him the child must move through the periods of intellectual development in an invariant order, and the chronological duration within each period is rather fixed, although there may be some compression or elongation due to the quality of the environment. For Skinner there is no such necessary structure at all: the order in which things are learned depends solely on the order in which they are encountered plus the operative contingencies of reinforcement.

Despite the differences just mentioned, there are some similarities between Piaget and Skinner. The main one is that both of their approaches are in at least one sense historical. That is to say, both believe behavior is progressively modified by environmental encounters and both concur that the direction of behavioral change is toward greater competence in dealing with the environment. However, Piaget places major emphasis on the interaction between an intrinsic maturational sequence and learning while Skinner focuses on the notion that appropriate reinforcement schedules simply change the probabilities that given responses will occur.

Comparing Piaget with Freud, Piaget apparently sees psychoanalytic theory as "a source of fruitful hypotheses." As was suggested in the dialogue, Piaget sees his own work within the same perspective. Another point of comparison is found in the fact that Piaget's notions of symbolic schemata are related to Freud's theories of primary-process thinking and dreams (Baldwin, 1968). Here they have used similar theoretical notions to investigate different problems. Thus, Piaget is interested in specific problems of conceptual thinking. Freud, of course, was greatly concerned with the way primary processes interfere with cognitive functioning. He concerned himself with the peculiar logic of dreams and neuroses, which is not unlike the conceptual thinking of young children. Moreover, Freud, just as Piaget, stressed a historical point of view, i.e., he emphasized that past events influence present behavior. An additional similarity between Piaget and Freud can be seen by comparing Freud's defense mechanism of identification with Piaget's use of imitation. Although obviously Freud's definition of identification is deeply embedded in affect, while to Piaget imitation is a more purely cognitive process, both concepts relate the infant's behavior development to a model in the environment.

Another apparent similarity might be the interest of both men in the development of morality. The introjection of threatening outside controls, taboos, and standards as well as innate taboos figures in Freud's theory of moral development, which also refers to a superego as an agent of this introjection. Piaget, however, tends to see a child's morality as being more autonomous and resulting from more spontaneous efforts to develop a moral code in the same sense as other reasoning processes develop. This results in an inner awareness relatively free from outside control or outside standards.

Finally, in comparing Piaget and Erikson, one sees an almost complete lack of similarity in their respective emphases, since Piaget focuses on intellect and Erikson on social-emotional considerations. Hence, it is often difficult to determine what ideas are generic to both of them. For example, Piaget labels the first stage of life as the sensory-motor period. To Erikson, this phase carries the label "phase of basic trust." Throughout their respective developmental models different descriptive terms are used. Thus, it becomes necessary to search beneath the semantic variations in their respective developmental models to grasp the essential ideas being conveyed. A clue to this is found in examining their respective views concerning when the child acts on or is acted upon by the environment. Piaget sees the operation of innate cognitive structures stimulated by the child's actions from the time of birth. Erikson views sociocultural and biological factors as codeterminants of the developmental process, but sees the child more as merely a "recipient" of these influences until it is several months of age.

However, there are areas of agreement between these two theorists. Both agree that the most favorable condition for studying the child's development is its natural environment, although they differ regarding the methodology of investigation and the particular developmental aspect (intellect versus social-emotional) to be stressed in investigations. Also, both theorists strongly believe that the child has the potential capacity to overcome obstacles, whether formed by it or its environment. Of course, as would be expected, each supports a different view as to how this happens, e.g., Piaget looks to the developing "logical" capacity of the maturing child, while Erikson focuses on the increasing social-emotional sensitivity of the maturing child. As suggested above, both theorists intricately describe the development of the child from birth through adolescence and perceive successful growth of the child from an earlier level to a more advanced level as crucial determiners of being a "successful" adult.

In summary, perhaps the most interesting point in comparing Piaget with Skinner, Freud, and Erikson is to stress the former's emphasis on the child as self-determined from the moment of birth. Of course, none of the other three envisions the child as *completely* passive. For example, Skinner would not regard his notion of operant conditioning as involving a purely passive subject in the sense that classical conditioning does. To Skinner, however, behavior modification results from arranged contingencies in a *controlled* environment, as he attempted to demonstrate by using the "Skinner Box" with the very young child. Erikson would contend that he does see the individual child as more of an actor *on* the environment at an earlier age than did Freud. But they clearly perceive the child as more subject to either biological and/or environmental vicissitudes than does Piaget. None of the three would appear to view the child as Piaget does: that even at birth it is already developing cognitive structures on the basis of what it does—spontaneously, necessarily, and innately.

JEAN PIAGET, AN AUTOBIOGRAPHY, AND LIST OF HIS MAJOR PUBLISHED WORKS

PART VIII

An autobiography has scientific interest only if it succeeds in furnishing the elements of an explanation of the author's work.[1] In order to achieve that goal, I shall therefore limit myself essentially to the scientific aspects of my life.

Many persons doubtless are convinced that such a retrospective interpretation presents no objective value, and that it is to be suspected of partiality even more than an introspective report. I myself had originally subscribed to this view. But, on rereading some old documents dating from my years of adolescence, I was struck by two apparently contradictory facts which, when put together, offer some guaranty of objectivity. The first is that I had completely forgotten the contents of these rather crude, juvenile productions; the second is that, in spite of their immaturity, they anticipated in a striking manner what I have been trying to do for about thirty years.

[1] Submitted in French and translated by Donald MacQueen of Clark University.

There is therefore probably some truth in the statement by Bergson that a philosophic mind is generally dominated by a single personal idea which he strives to express in many ways in the course of his life, without ever succeeding fully. Even if this autobiography should not convey to the readers a perfectly clear notion of what that single idea is, it will at least have helped the author to understand it better himself.

I. 1896–1914

I was born on August 9, 1896, at Neuchâtel, in Switzerland. My father, who is still active, has devoted his writings mostly to medieval literature, and to a lesser extent, to the history of Neuchâtel. He is a man of a painstaking and critical mind, who dislikes hastily improvised generalizations, and is not afraid of starting a fight when he finds historic truth twisted to fit respectable traditions. Among many other things he taught me the value of systematic work, even in small matters. My mother was very intelligent, energetic, and fundamentally a very kind person; her rather neurotic temperament, however, made our family life somewhat troublesome. One of the direct consequences of this situation was that I started to forgo playing for serious work very early; this I obviously did as much to imitate my father as to take refuge in both a private and a nonfictitious world. Indeed, I have always detested any departure from reality, an attitude which I relate to the second important influential factor of my early life, viz., my mother's poor mental health; it was this disturbing factor which at the beginning of my studies in psychology made me intensely interested in questions of psychoanalysis and pathological psychology. Though this interest helped me to achieve independence and to widen my cultural background, I have never since felt any desire to involve myself deeper in that particular direction, always much preferring the study of normality and of the workings of the intellect to that of the tricks of the unconscious.

From seven to ten years of age I became successively interested in mechanics, in birds, in fossils of secondary and tertiary layers, and in seashells. Since I was not yet allowed to write with ink, I composed (in pencil) a little pamphlet to share with the world a great discovery: the "autovap," an automobile provided with a steam engine. But I quickly forgot this unusual combination of a wagon and a locomotive for the writing (this time in ink) of a book on "Our Birds," which, after my father's ironic remarks, I had to recognize, regretfully, as a mere compilation.

At the age of ten, as soon as I had entered "Latin School," I decided to be more serious. Having seen a partly albino sparrow in a public park, I sent a one-page article to a natural history journal of Neuchâtel. It published my lines and I was "launched!" I wrote then to the director of the Musée d'histoire naturelle and asked his permission to study his collections of birds, fossils, and shells after hours. This director, Paul Godet, a very nice man, happened to be a great specialist on mollusks. He immediately invited me to assist him twice a week—as he said, like the "famulus"

to Faust—helping him stick labels on his collections of
land- and soft-water shells. For four years I worked
for this conscientious and learned naturalist, in exchange for which he would give me at the end of each
session a certain number of rare species for my own
collection and, in particular, provide me with an exact
classification of the samples that I had collected. These
weekly meetings in the director's private office stimulated me so much that I spent all my free time collecting mollusks (there are one hundred and thirty species
and hundreds of varieties in the environs of Neuchâtel); every Saturday afternoon I used to wait for
my teacher a half hour ahead of time!

This early initiation to malacology had a great influence on me. When, in 1911, Mr. Godet died, I
knew enough about this field to begin publishing
without help (specialists in this branch are rare) a
series of articles on the mollusks of Switzerland, of
Savoy, of Brittany, and even of Colombia. This
afforded me some amusing experiences. Certain for-
eign "colleagues" wanted to meet me, but since I was
only a schoolboy, I didn't dare to show myself and had
to decline these flattering invitations. The director of
the Musée d'histoire naturelle of Geneva, Mr. Bedot,
who was publishing several of my articles in the *Revue
suisse de Zoologie* offered me a position as curator of
his mollusk collection. (The Lamarck collection,
among others, is in Geneva.) I had to reply that I had
two more years to study for my baccalaureate degree,
not yet being a college student. After another magazine
editor had refused an article of mine because he had
discovered the embarrassing truth about my age, I

sent it to Mr. Bedot who with kindness and good humor responded: "It is the first time that I have even heard of a magazine director who judges the value of articles by the age of their authors. Can it be that he has no other criteria at his disposal?" Naturally, these various articles which I published at such a young age were far from being accomplished feats. It was only much later, in 1929, that I was able to achieve something more significant in this field.

These studies, premature as they were, were nevertheless of great value for my scientific development; moreover, they functioned, if I may say so, as instruments of protection against the demon of philosophy. Thanks to them, I had the rare privilege of getting a glimpse of science and what it stands for, before undergoing the philosophical crises of adolescence. To have had early experience with these two kinds of problematic approaches constituted, I am certain, the hidden strength of my later psychological activity.

However, instead of quietly pursuing the career of a naturalist, which seemed so normal and so easy for me after these fortunate circumstances, between the ages of fifteen and twenty, I experienced a series of crises due both to family conditions and to the intellectual curiosity characteristic of that productive age. But, I repeat, all those crises I was able to overcome, thanks to the mental habits which I had acquired through early contact with the zoological science.

There was the problem of religion. When I was about fifteen, my mother, being a devout Protestant, insisted on my taking what is called at Neuchâtel "religious instruction," that is, a six-weeks' course on the fundamentals of Christian doctrine. My father, on the other hand, did not attend church, and I quickly sensed that for him the current faith and an honest historical criticism were incompatible. Accordingly I followed my "religious instruction" with lively interest but, at the same time, in the spirit of freethinking. Two things struck me at that time: on the one hand, the difficulty of reconciling a number of dogmas with biology, and on the other, the fragility of the "five" proofs of the existence of God. We were taught five, and I even passed my examination in them! Though I would not even have dreamed of denying the existence of God, the fact that anyone should reason by such weak arguments (I recall only the proof by the finality of nature and the ontological proof) seemed to me all the more extraordinary since my pastor was an intelligent man, who himself dabbled in the natural sciences!

At that time I had the good luck to find in my father's library *La philosophie de la religion fondée sur la psychologie et l'histoire* by Auguste Sabatier. I devoured that book with immense delight. Dogmas reduced to the function of "symbols," necessarily inadequate, and above all the notion of an "evolution of dogmas"—there was a language which was much more understandable and satisfactory to my mind. And now a new passion took possession of me: philosophy.

From this a second crisis ensued. My godfather, Samuel Cornut, a Romanish man of letters, invited me about that same period to spend a vacation with him at Lake Annecy. I still have a delightful memory of that visit: We walked and fished, I looked for mollusks and wrote a "malacology of Lake Annecy," which I published shortly afterward in the *Revue savoisienne*. But my godfather had a purpose. He found me too specialized and wanted to teach me philosophy. Between the gatherings of mollusks he would teach me the "creative evolution" of Bergson. (It was only afterward that he sent me that work as a souvenir.) It was the first time that I heard philosophy discussed by anyone not a theologian; the shock was terrific, I must admit.

First of all, it was an emotional shock. I recall one evening of profound revelation. The identification of God with life itself was an idea that stirred me almost to ecstasy because it now enabled me to see in biology the explanation of all things and of the mind itself.

In the second place, it was an intellectual shock. The problem of knowing (properly called the epistemological problem) suddenly appeared to me in an entirely new perspective and as an absorbing topic of study. It made me decide to consecrate my life to the biological explanation of knowledge.

The reading of Bergson himself, which I did only several months later (I have always preferred to reflect on a problem before reading on it), strengthened me in my decision but also disappointed me somewhat. Instead of finding science's last word therein, as my good godfather had led me to hope, I got the impression of an ingenious construction without an experimental basis: Between biology and the analysis of knowledge I needed something other than a philosophy. I believe it was at that moment that I discovered a need that could be satisfied only by psychology.

II. 1914–1918

It was during this period that the curious phenomenon to which I alluded in my introduction began
to happen. Not being satisfied with reading a lot (this
in addition to the study on mollusks and preparation
for the baccalaureate degree which I received in 1915
at the age of eighteen), I began to write down my own
ideas in numerous notebooks. Soon these efforts affected my health; I had to spend more than a year
in the mountains filling my enforced leisure time with
writing a sort of philosophic novel which I was im-
prudent enough to publish in 1917. Now, in reading
over these various writings which mark the crisis and
the end of my adolescence—documents which I had
completely forgotten till I reopened them for this
autobiography—surprisingly I find in them one or two
ideas which are still dear to me, and which have never
ceased to guide me in my variegated endeavors. That
is why, however unworthy such attempt may seem at
first, I shall try to retrace these early notions.

I began by reading everything which came to my
hands after my unfortunate contact with the philosophy of Bergson: some Kant, Spencer, Auguste Comte,
Fouillée and Guyau, Lachelier, Boutroux, Lalande,
Durkheim, Tarde, Le Dantec; and, in psychology,
W. James, Th. Ribot, and Janet. Also, during the last
two years before the baccalaureate, we had lessons in
psychology, in logic, and in scientific methodology
given by the logician, A. Reymond. But for lack of a
laboratory and guidance (there was no experimental

psychologist at Neuchâtel, even at the university) the only thing I could do was to theorize and write. I wrote even if it was only for myself, for I could not think without writing—but it had to be in a systematic fashion as if it were to be an article for publication.

I started with a rather crudely conceived essay pretentiously entitled "Sketch of a Neo-Pragmatism"; here I presented an idea which has since remained central for me, namely, that action in itself admits of logic (this contrary to the anti-intellectualism of James and of Bergson) and that, therefore, logic stems from a sort of spontaneous organization of acts. But the link with biology was missing. A lesson by A. Reymond on realism and nominalism within the problem area of "universals" (with some reference to the role of concepts in present-day science) gave me a sudden insight. I had thought deeply on the problem of "species" in zoology and had adopted an entirely nominalistic point of view in this respect. The species has no reality in itself and is distinguished from the simple "varieties" merely by a greater stability. But this theoretical view, inspired by Lamarckism, bothered me somewhat in my empirical work (viz., classification of mollusks). The dispute of Durkheim and Tarde on the reality or nonreality of society as an organized whole plunged me into a similar state of uncertainty without making me see, at first, its pertinence to the problem of the species. Aside from this, the general problem of realism and of nominalism provided me with an overall view: I suddenly understood that at all levels (viz., that of the living cell, organism, species, society, etc., but also with reference to states of conscience, to concepts, to logical principles, etc.) one finds the same problem of relationship between the parts and the whole; hence I was convinced that I had found the solution. There at last was the close union that I had dreamed of between biology and philosophy, there was an access to an epistemology which to me then seemed really scientific!

Thus I began to write down my system (people will wonder where I got the time, but I took it wherever I could, especially during boring lessons!). My solution was very simple: In all fields of life (organic, mental, social) there exist "totalities" qualitatively distinct from their parts and imposing on them an organization. Therefore there exist no isolated "elements"; elementary reality is necessarily dependent on a whole which pervades it. But the relationships between the whole and the part vary from one structure to another, for it is necessary to distinguish four actions which are always present: the action of the whole on itself (preservation), the action of all the parts (alteration or preservation), the actions of the parts on themselves (preservation) and the action of the parts on the whole (alteration or preservation). These four actions balance one another in a total structure; but there are then three possible forms of equilibrium: (1) predominance of the whole with alteration of the parts; (2) predominance of the parts with alteration of the whole; and (3) reciprocal preservation of the parts and of the whole. To this a final fundamental law is added: Only the last form of equilibrium (3) is "stable" or "good," while the other two, (1) and (2), are less stable; though tending toward stability, it will depend on the obstacles to be overcome how closely (1) and (2) may approach a stable status.

If I had known at that time (1913–1915) the work of Wertheimer and of Köhler, I would have become a Gestaltist; but having been acquainted only with French writings and not yet able to design experiments for the verification of these hypotheses, I was bound to limit myself to the construction of a system. I find the rereading of these old papers extremely interesting, inasmuch as they represent an anticipatory outline of my later research. It was already clear to me that the stable equilibrium of the whole and of the parts (third form) corresponded to states of conscience of a normative nature: logical necessity or moral obligation, as opposed to inferior forms of equilibrium which characterize the non-normative states of conscience, such as perception, etc., or organismic happenings.

After my baccalaureate, I took to the mountains for a rest. During that time I was formally registered in the Division of Science at the University of Neuchâtel, so that, soon after my return, I was able to graduate in the natural sciences and then to take my doctor's degree with a thesis on the mollusks of Valais (1918). Though I was all the while greatly interested in courses in zoology (Fuhrmann), embryology (Béraneck), geology (Argand), physical chemistry (Berthoud), and mathematics (group theory was particularly important for me with respect to the problem of the whole and the parts), I was very eager to move to a larger university with a psychology laboratory where I could hope to carry out experiments to verify my "system."

It was in this area of research where the mental

habits acquired from contact with zoology were to serve me well. I never believed in a system without precise experimental control. What I wrote for myself during my years at the lycée I deemed unworthy of publication, because it remained mere theory; its real value seemed to me to be an incentive for later experiments, whose nature at that time, however, I could not surmise.

Nevertheless, during the year I spent in the mountains I was haunted by the desire to create, and I yielded to the temptation. Not to compromise myself on scientific grounds, however, I avoided the difficulty by writing—for the general public, and not for specialists—a kind of philosophic novel, the last part of which contained my ideas (1917). My strategy proved to be correct: No one spoke of it except one or two indignant philosophers.[2]

[2] Here are some quotations from that work entitled *Recherche* (1917). It was a question of elaborating a "positive theory of quality taking into account only relationships of equilibrium and disequilibrium among our qualities" (p. 150). "Now there can be no awareness of these qualities, hence these qualities cannot exist, if there are no relationships among them, if they are not, consequently, blended into a total quality which contains them while keeping them distinct. For example, I would not be aware either of the whiteness of this paper or of the blackness of this ink if the two qualities were not combined in my consciousness into a certain unit, and if, in spite of this unity, they did not remain respectively one white and the other black. . . . In this originates the equilibrium between the qualities: there is equilibrium not only among the separate parts in that way (and that occurs only in material equilibriums) but among the parts on the one hand, and the whole on the other, as distinct from the whole resulting from these partial qualities. . . . (It is therefore necessary to proceed from the whole to the parts and not from the part to the whole as does a physicist's mind)" (pp. 151–153). "One can then distinguish

III. 1918–1921

After having received the doctorate in the sciences, I left for Zurich (1918), with the aim of working in a psychology laboratory. I attended two laboratories, that of G. E. Lipps and that of Wreschner, and also Bleuler's psychiatric clinic. I felt at once that there lay my path and that, in utilizing for psychological experimentation the mental habits I had acquired in zoology, I would perhaps succeed in solving problems of structures-of-the-whole to which I had been led by my philosophical thinking. But to tell the truth, I felt somewhat lost at first. The experiments of Lipps and Wreschner seemed to me to have little bearing on fundamental problems. On the other hand, the discovery of psychoanalysis (I read Freud and the journal *Imago,* and listened occasionally to Pfister's and Jung's lectures) and the teachings of Bleuler made me sense the danger of solitary meditation; I decided then to forget my system lest I should fall a victim to "autism."

---

a first type of equilibrium where the whole and the part mutually sustain each other" (p. 156), and other types such that there be coordinated interaction between the whole and the parts (p. 157). Now "all equilibriums tend toward an equilibrium of the first type" (p. 157), but without being able to reach it on the organic level: "Therefore we call an ideal equilibrium the equilibrium of the first type and real equilibrium that of the other types, although every real equilibrium, whatever it be, presupposes an ideal equilibrium" (p. 158). In contrast, the first type is realized on the level of thought: It is "the origin of the principle of identity, from which the principle of contradiction is deduced," etc. (p. 163).

In the spring of 1919 I became restless and left for le Valais; there I applied Lipps's statistical method to a biometric study of the variability of land mollusks as a function of altitude! I needed to get back to concrete problems to avoid grave errors.

In the autumn of 1919 I took the train for Paris where I spent two years at the Sorbonne. I attended Dumas' course in pathological psychology (where I learned to interview mental patients at Sainte-Anne), and the courses of Piéron and Delacroix; I also studied logic and philosophy of science with Lalande and Brunschwieg. The latter exerted a great influence on me because of his historical-critical method and his references to psychology. But I still did not know what problem area of experimentation to choose. Then I had an extraordinary piece of luck. I was recommended to Dr. Simon who was then living in Rouen, but who had at his disposal Binet's laboratory at the grade school of the rue de la Grangeaux-Belles in Paris. This laboratory was not being used because Simon had no classes in Paris at this time. Dr. Simon received me in a very friendly manner and suggested that I should standardize Burt's reasoning tests on the Parisian children. I started the work without much enthusiasm, just to try anything. But soon my mood changed; there I was, my own master, with a whole school at my disposition—unhoped-for working conditions.

Now from the very first questionings I noticed that though Burt's tests certainly had their diagnostic merits, based on the number of successes and failures, it was much more interesting to try to find the reasons

for the failures. Thus I engaged my subjects in conversations patterned after psychiatric questioning, with
the aim of discovering something about the reasoning
process underlying their right, but especially their
wrong answers. I noticed with amazement that the
simplest reasoning task involving the inclusion of a
part in the whole or the coordination of relations or the
"multiplication" of classes (finding the part common to
two wholes) presented for normal children up to the
age of eleven or twelve difficulties unsuspected by the
adult.

Without Dr. Simon being quite aware of what I was
doing, I continued for about two years to analyze the
verbal reasoning of normal children by presenting
them with various questions and exposing them to
tasks involving simple concrete relations of cause and
effect. Furthermore, I obtained permission to work
with the abnormal children of the Salpétrière; here I
undertook research on numbers, using the methods of
direct manipulation as well as that of conversation.
I have since resumed this work in cooperation with
A. Szeminska.*

At last I had found my field of research. First of all
it became clear to me that the theory of the relations
between the whole and the part can be studied experimentally through analysis of the psychological
processes underlying logical operations. This marked
the end of my "theoretical" period and the start of an
inductive and experimental era in the psychological
domain which I always had wanted to enter, but for

* Piaget, Szeminska, and Inhelder *La géométrie spontanée
chez l'enfant* (Paris: P. U. F., 1948).

which until then I had not found the suitable problems. Thus my observations that logic is not inborn, but develops little by little, appeared to be consistent with my ideas on the formation of the equilibrium toward which the evolution of mental structures tends; moreover, the possibility of directly studying the problem of logic was in accord with all my former philosophical interests. Finally my aim of discovering a sort of embryology of intelligence fit in with my biological training; from the start of my theoretical thinking I was certain that the problem of the relation between the organism and environment extended also into the realm of knowledge, appearing here as the problem of the relation between the acting or thinking subject and the objects of his experience. Now I had the chance of studying this problem in terms of psychogenetic development.

Once my first results had been achieved, I wrote three articles, taking great care not to become biased by theory. I analyzed the data, psychologically as well as logically, applying the principle of logical-psychological parallelism to my method of analysis: Psychology explains the facts in terms of causality, while logic when concerned with true reasoning describes the corresponding forms in terms of an ideal equilibrium[3] (I have since expressed this relation by saying that logic is the axiomatic whose corresponding experimental science is the psychology of thought).[4]

[3] Cf. "Une forme verbale de la comparaison chez l'enfant," Arch. de Psychol. (1921), 18, 143–172.
[4] Psychologie de l'intelligence (1947), Chap. 1.

I sent my first article[5] to the *Journal de Psychologie* and had the pleasure not only of seeing it accepted, but also of noting that I. Meyerson who became my friend at this time had interests very similar to mine. He had me read Lévy-Bruhl and spurred me on by his encouragement and advice. He also accepted my second article.[6]

As for the third, I sent it to Ed. Claparède, whom I had met but once, and who published it in the *Archives de Psychologie*.[7] But in addition to accepting my article, he made a proposal which changed the course of my life. He offered me the job of "director of studies" at the Institut J. J. Rousseau of Geneva. Since he barely knew me, he asked me to come to Geneva for a month's trial. This prospect enchanted me, as much because of Claparède's fame as for the wonderful research facilities which this position would afford; on the other hand, as yet I did not know how to start out on any research! I accepted in principle, and left Paris for Geneva. I noted immediately that Claparède and Bovet were ideal *patrons* who would let me work according to my desires. My work consisted simply of guiding the students and of associating them with the research that I was asked to undertake on my own, provided it was in child psychology. This was in 1921.

[5] "Essai sur quelques aspects du développement de la notion de partie chez l'enfant," *J. de Psychol.* (1921), 38, 449–480.

[6] "Essai sur la multiplication logique et les débuts de la pensées formelles chez l'enfant," *J. de Psychol.* (1922), 38, 222–261.

[7] "La pensée symbolique et la pensée chez l'enfant," *Arch. de Psychol.* (1923), 38, 273–304.

IV. 1921–1925

Being of a systematic turn of mind (with all the hazards that this implies), I made plans which I then considered final: I would devote two or three years more to the study of child thought, then return to the origins of mental life, that is, study the emergence of intelligence during the first two years. After having thus gained objectively and inductively a knowledge about the elementary structures of intelligence, I would be in the position to attack the problem of thought in general and to construct a psychological and biological epistemology. Above all, then, I would have to stay away from any nonpsychological preoccupation and study empirically the development of thought for itself, wherever this might lead me.

According to this plan I organized my research at the Maison des Petits of the Institut J. J. Rousseau, starting with the more peripheral factors (social environment, language), but keeping in mind my goal of getting at the psychological mechanism of logical operations and of causal reasoning. In this connection I also resumed working with the primary school pupils of Geneva, the type of investigation I had done in Paris.

The results of the research is contained in my first five books on child psychology.[8] I published them

[8] *The Language and Thought of the Child* (1924), *The Child's Conception of the World* (1926), *The Child's Conception of Causality* (1927), *Judgment and Reasoning in the Child* (1928), *The Moral Judgment of the Child* (1932).

without taking sufficient precautions concerning the presentation of my conclusions, thinking they would be little read and would serve me mainly as documentation for a later synthesis to be addressed to a wider audience. (The studies were the product of a continuous collaborative effort in which all students of the Institut participated, among them Valentine Châtenay who became my wife and constant coworker.) Contrary to my expectation, the books were read and discussed as if they were my last word on the subject, some adopting my point of view of a genesis of logic, others strongly opposing it (especially in circles influenced by empirical epistemology or Thomism). I was invited to many countries (France, Belgium, the Netherlands, England, Scotland, the United States, Spain, Poland, etc.) to present my ideas and discuss them before university faculties and other teachers. (However, I had no interest in pedagogy at that time as I had no children.) This unexpected acclaim left me somewhat uneasy, since I realized quite clearly that as yet I had not organized my ideas and had barely entered the preliminaries. But one cannot say to the critics, "Wait—you have not seen what is coming"—especially when one does not know it himself. Besides, when one is young he does not suspect that, for a long time, he will be judged by his first works, and that only very conscientious people will read the later ones.

Two essential shortcomings existed in these first studies. One I was not aware of before studying infant behavior; the other, however, I knew perfectly well.

The first of these shortcomings consisted in limiting

my research to language and expressed thought. I well knew that thought proceeds from action, but I believed then that language directly reflects acts and that to understand the logic of the child one had only to look for it in the domain of conversations or verbal interactions. It was only later, by studying the patterns of intelligent behavior of the first two years, that I learned that for a complete understanding of the genesis of intellectual operations, manipulation and experience with objects had first to be considered. Therefore, prior to study based on verbal conversations, an examination of the patterns of conduct had to be carried out. True enough, since one finds in the action of younger children all the characteristics he observes in the verbal behavior of older children, my first studies on verbal thought were not in vain; but my point of view would have been much more easily understood if I had found out then what I discovered only later: that, between the preoperative stage from two to seven years and the establishment of a formal logic occurring at the ages of eleven and twelve, there functions (between seven and eleven years of age) an organizational level of "concrete operations" which is essentially logical, though not yet formal-logical (for instance, the child of eight will be able to conclude $A < C$ if he has seen three objects under the form $B > A$ and $B < C$, but he will fail to perform the same operation on the purely verbal plane).

The second shortcoming stems from the first, but I did not quite understand the reasons then: I tried in vain to find characteristic structures-of-the-whole relative to logical operations themselves (again my theory of the part and the whole!); I did not succeed because I did not seek their source in concrete operations. So I satisfied my need for an explanation in terms of structures-of-the-whole by studying the social aspect of thought (which is a necessary aspect, I still believe, of the formation of logical operations as such). The ideal equilibrium (the reciprocal preservation of the whole and of the parts) pertains here to the cooperation between individuals who become autonomous by this very cooperation. Imperfect equilibrium characterized by the alteration of the parts in relation to the whole appears here as social constraint (or constraint of the younger by the older). Imperfect equilibrium characterized by the change of the whole as a function of the parts (and the lack of coordination of the parts) appears as unconscious egocentricity of the individual, that is, as the mental attitude of young children who do not yet know how to collaborate or to coordinate their points of view. (Unfortunately, because of the vague definition of the term "egocentricity"—undoubtedly an ill-chosen term! —and because of the misunderstandings of the concept of mental attitude, this term has usually not been given its only clear and simple meaning.)

Though I failed at first to find the characteristic structures of logical operations which ought to correspond to the structures of social intercourse (at least I sensed at once the importance of the reversibility of thought),[9] I noticed that a certain degree of irrevers-

[9] *Judgment and Reasoning in the Child* (1928), p. 169.

ibility of operations corresponded to the young child's difficulties in grasping intellectual and social reciprocity. But to put this hypothesis on solid ground I had first to study concrete operations.

During these years, I had discovered the existence of Gestalt psychology, so close to my notions concerning structures-of-the-whole. The contact with the work of Köhler and Wertheimer made a twofold impression on me. Firstly, I had the pleasure of concluding that my previous research was not sheer folly, since one could design on such a central hypothesis of the subordination of the parts to the organizing whole not only a consistent theory, but also a splendid series of experiments. In the second place, I felt that, though the Gestalt notion suited perfectly the inferior forms of equilibrium (those in which the part is altered by the whole or those in which, according to the very terms of the theory, there is no "additive composition"), it did not explain the kind of structure peculiar to logical or rational operations. For example, the sequence of whole numbers $1, 2, 3 \ldots$ etc. is a remarkable, operative structure-of-the-whole, since numbers do not exist alone but are engendered by the very law of formation itself ($1 + 1 = 2, 2 + 1 = 3$, etc.). And yet this law of formation constitutes essentially an "additive composition." What I consider a superior form of equilibrium (the mutual preservation of the parts by the whole and of the whole by the parts) therefore escaped the Gestaltist explanation. From this I concluded that it was necessary to differentiate successive steps of equilibriums and to integrate the search for types of structures with a more genetic approach.

V. 1925–1929

In 1925 my former teacher, A. Reymond, vacated his chair of philosophy at the University of Neuchâtel, and a part of its incumbency was given to me, though I was merely a doctor of sciences. (Since 1921, as *privat-dozent* in the Faculté des Sciences at Geneva, I also taught child psychology.) My duties at this time were very heavy: They included (in the Faculté des Lettres) the teaching of psychology, of philosophy of science, of a philosophy seminar, and also, of two hours of sociology at the Institut des Sciences Sociales. In addition I continued to teach child psychology at the Institut J. J. Rousseau. Since one learns by teaching, I expected that this heavy schedule would at least bring me closer to epistemology. In fact, for four years I devoted the course on philosophy of science to the study of the development of ideas as it can be observed in the history of science as well as in child psychology. The opening lecture on this subject[10] has since been published.

During these years many other problems occupied me. In 1925 my first daughter was born and my second in 1927 (a boy followed them in 1931). With the help of my wife I spent considerable time in observing their reactions, and also subjected them to various experiments. The results of this new research

[10] "Psychologie et critique de la connaissance," *Arch. de Psychol.* (1925), 19, 193–210.

has been published in three volumes that deal mainly
with the genesis of intelligent conduct, ideas of objective constancy and causality, and with the beginnings
of symbolic behavior (imitation and play).[11] It is
not feasible to summarize these books; the first two
have not been published in English, but the third
(written much later) is now in the process of being
translated.

The main benefit which I derived from these studies
was that I learned in the most direct way how intellectual operations are prepared by sensory-motor action, even before the appearance of language. I concluded that in order to progress in my research on
child logic I had to change my method, or rather to
modify it by directing the conversations toward objects which the child himself could manipulate.

In the course of experiments (undertaken in collaboration with my students at Neuchâtel and at
Geneva), I had just discovered that children up to
twelve years did not believe in the constancy of
material quantity, e.g., of the weight and the volume
of a lump of modeling clay that changed its shape
by stretching or flattening. I had observed in my own
children that between the sixth and tenth month they
did not possess the notion of the permanence of an
object disappearing from view (a watch hidden
beneath a handkerchief, etc.). Between the beginnings of a notion of constancy or permanence of concrete objects and the final mastery of the concept of

---

[11] *La naissance de l'intelligence chez l'enfant* (1937); *La
construction du réel chez l'enfant* (1937); *La formation du
symbole chez l'enfant* (1945).

constancy of physical properties (weight, mass, etc.), there had to be successive stages in the development of ideas of constancy which could be studied in concrete situations rather than solely through language. Experiments on this problem I resumed again much later, after my return to Geneva, in collaboration with A. Szeminska and B. Inhelder.

Before leaving Neuchâtel, I concluded the research on mollusks by clearing up a question which had preoccupied me for many years, and which touched on the fundamental problem of the relation between hereditary structure and environment. Indeed, this last problem had always seemed to me to be central, not only for the genetic classification of organic forms (morphogeny), but also for psychological learning theory (maturation versus learning) and epistemology. Therefore it seemed worthwhile to me to utilize my zoological findings for studying, in however limited a way, that significant problem of morphogenesis. I have been aware of a variety of *Limnaea stagnalis* particularly abundant in the lake of Neuchâtel and remarkable for its adaptation to its environment. Its globular shape comes from the action of the waves which constantly force the animal to clamp itself to the stones, and thus cause an enlargement of the opening and shortening of the whorl during the period of growth. The problem was to determine whether these traits were hereditary. Observations on eighty thousand individuals living in their natural environment and on many thousands grown in an aquarium led me to draw the following conclusions: (1) this variety exists only in large lakes and in those sections of the lakes where the water is roughest; (2) its traits are hereditary and survive in an aquarium after five or six generations; a pure species can be segregated which reproduces according to the Mendelian laws of crossbreeding. The variety is able to live outside the lakes; I deposited some of them in a pond where they are still thriving after twenty years. The hypothesis of chance mutation, independent of environmental stimulation, seems unlikely in this particular case, since nothing prevents this globular variety from living in any body of fresh water.[12] That experience has taught me not to explain the whole of mental life by maturation alone!

VI. 1929–1939

In 1929 I returned to the University of Geneva as Professor of History of Scientific Thought (in the Division of Science) and Assistant Director of the Institut J. J. Rousseau; in 1932 I became codirector, with Claparède and Bovet. [For a few years after] 1936 I also taught experimental psychology at the University of Lausanne one day a week. In addition, in 1929 I imprudently accepted the duties of director of the Bureau International Office de l'Education on the insistence of my friend Pedro Rossello, who had be-

[12] See "Les races lacustres de la *Limnaea stagnalis*, L. Recherches sur les rapports de l'adaptation héréditaire avec le milieu," *Bull. biol. de la France et de la Belgique* (1929), 18, 424–455; and "L'adaptation de la *Limnaea stagnalis* aux milieux lacustres de la Suisse romande," *Rev. suisse de Zool.* (1929), 36, Plates 3–6, 263–531.

come its assistant director. For two reasons this international office, which now is working in close collaboration with UNESCO, interested me. In the first place it was able, through its intergovernmental organization, to contribute toward the improvement of pedagogical methods and toward the official adoption of techniques better adapted to the mentality of the child. Secondly, there was, so to speak, an element of sport in that venture. Rossello and I had succeeded in having accepted a new organization essentially on an intergovernmental basis. But on the day the statute was signed there were only three governments participating: the canton of Geneva (the Swiss government itself was represented but undecided), Poland, and Ecuador. Moreover we were the subject of poorly repressed opposition (I am speaking to psychologists!) by the Institut de Coopération Intellectuelle. We had to act quickly and with diplomacy. A few years later between thirty-five and forty-five governments were represented at the annual conferences called by the Swiss government (today this organization is sponsored jointly by UNESCO and the International Office of Education). This job has certainly cost me a good deal of time I might possibly have spent more advantageously on research in child psychology, but at least I have learned from it quite a bit about adult psychology!

Added to these nonscientific labors were other administrative duties; I had in particular the task of reorganizing the Institut J. J. Rousseau which ceased to be private and became partially affiliated with the university.

The years from 1929 to 1939 cover a period filled with scientific endeavors. Three principal events stand out in retrospect.

First, the course in the History of Scientific Thought which I gave in the Faculté des Sciences at Geneva enabled me to promote more vigorously the project of a scientific epistemology founded on mental development, both autogenetic and phylogenetic. For ten successive years I studied intensely the emergence and history of the principal concepts of mathematics, physics, and biology.

Second, I again resumed, on a larger scale than before, the research in child psychology at the Institut J. J. Rousseau. This work I carried out in collaboration with most able assistants, particularly A. Szeminska, and B. Inhelder, who now occupies the chair of child psychology. Thanks to them, a series of new experiments could be performed that dealt systematically with problems of action (manipulation of objects), whereby the conversation that was carried on with the subject exclusively involved the child's own manipulatory conduct. By this method I studied the development of numbers with A. Szeminska, that of the ideas of physical quantity with B. Inhelder; I also started studies of spatial, temporal, and other relationships with E. Meyer. The most advanced of these studies were published around 1940,[13] at a time when psychologists no longer had the opportunity of ex-

[13] Piaget and A. Szeminska, La genèse du nombre chez l'enfant (1941); Piaget and B. Inhelder, Le développement des quantités chez l'enfant (1941). La genèse du nombre will soon be translated into English.

changing their ideas across frontiers, or often, even of doing research. Thus these books were little read outside of French-speaking areas, though they were the first to develop fully a number of problems on which my first books hardly had touched.

Third, the study of concrete operations finally enabled me to discover the operative structures-of-the-whole that I had been seeking so long. I analyzed in children four to seven or eight years of age the relationship of part and whole (by asking them to add pearls to a group of predetermined magnitude), the sequences of asymmetrical relationships (by letting them construct series of prescribed order), and the correspondences, item by item (by making them build two or more corresponding rows), etc. These studies led me to understand why logical and mathematical operations cannot be formed independently: The child can grasp a certain operation only if he is capable, at the same time, of correlating operations by modifying them in different, well-determined ways— for instance, by inverting them. These operations presuppose, as does any primary intelligent conduct, the possibility of making detours (which corresponds to what logicians call "associativity") and returns ("reversibility"). Thus the operations always represent reversible structures which depend on a total system that, in itself, may be entirely additive. Certain of these more complex structures-of-the-whole have been studied in mathematics under the name of "groups" and "lattices"; operative systems of this sort are indeed of importance for the development of equilibriums of thought. I sought for the most elementary operative structures-of-the-whole, and I finally found them in the mental processes underlying the formation of the idea of preservation or constancy. Simpler than the "groups" and the "lattices," such structures represent the most primitive parts of a part-whole organization: I have called them "groupings." For example, a classification (whereby the classes of the same rank order are always discrete and separate) is a grouping.

I presented my first paper on this subject, although I had not yet thoroughly mastered it, at the International Congress of Psychology at Paris in 1937. At that same time I was trying to determine the logical structure of groupings of classes and relationships of which I was able to isolate eight interdependent forms. I wrote an article in 1939 on this topic which P. Guillaume and I. Meyerson published in their "Collection Psychologique and Philosophique."[14]

VII. 1939–1950

The war spared Switzerland without our really knowing exactly why. However great his concern, an intellectual of my age (forty-three years), no longer subject to military service (I had been definitely released in 1916), could possess his arms or go on with his work.

When the professor of sociology at the University of Geneva gave up his position in 1939, I was, without

[14] *Classes, relations et nombres. Essai sur la réversibilité de la pensée* (1942).

my knowledge, nominated to that post; I accepted the call. A few months later Claparède fell ill of a disease which was to be fatal; I took over his duties, and in 1940 was given the chair of Experimental Psychology and named Director of the Psychology Laboratory (there I found an outstanding coworker in Lambercier). I continued editing the *Archives de Psychologie*, first with Rey, and later with Rey and Lambercier. A Swiss Society of Psychology was founded shortly thereafter and I assumed the presidency of it for the first three years, collaborating with Morgenthaler in editing a new *Revue Suisse de Psychologie*. There was much work to be done.

From 1939 to 1945 I carried on two kinds of research. Firstly, on assuming the responsibility of the laboratory made famous by the names of Th. Flournoy and Ed. Claparède, I undertook, with the collaboration of Lambercier* and various assistants, a long-range study on the development of perceptions in the child (until the age of adulthood). The aim of this study was to better understand the relationship of perception and intelligence, as well as to test the claims of the Gestalt theory (which had not convinced me with respect to the problem of intelligence). The first results of this research, which we are still continuing, have already appeared in the *Archives de Psychologie*;[15] they seem to us rather instructive for a

* Work on Perception, 1942–1958; culminated with book, J. Piaget, *Les Mécanismes Perceptifs* (Paris: Presses Universitaires de Gravee, 1961).

[15] "Recherches sur le développement des perceptions" (Recherches I à XII), *Arch. de Psychol.* (1942–1950).

theory of structure. Whereas logical structures deal only with one of the various aspects of the objects (class, number, size, weight, etc.), but, as far as that aspect is concerned, are complete, the perceptual structures are for the most part incomplete because they are statistical or merely probable. It is because of this character of probability that the perceptual structures are not additive, but follow the Gestalt laws. These structures do not remain the same at all ages: They have a less active character in the child than in the adult, and are closer to the products of intelligence in the latter. These facts are of consequence in such matters as the degree of geometric-optical illusions as a function of age, the magnitude of perceptual constancy, etc.

Secondly, by utilizing a concrete experimental technique and analytical method of procedure, and with the assistance of many collaborators, I began research on the development of ideas of time, of movement, of velocity, as well as on behavior involving these concepts.[16]

In 1942 Piéron was kind enough to invite me to give a series of lectures at the Collège de France; that occasion enabled me to bring to our French colleagues— it was during the German occupation—testimony of the unshakable affection of their friends from outside. The main content of these lectures appeared shortly after the war in a small volume which is now available in English[17] as well as in German, Swedish, etc.

[16] *Le développement de la notion de temps chez l'enfant. Les notions de mouvement et de vitesse chez l'enfant* (1946).
[17] Piaget, *The Psychology of Intelligence* (1950).

As soon as the war was over, social exchanges were resumed with renewed effort. The International Office of Education had never completely ceased to function during the years 1939 to 1945; it had served particularly as a clearinghouse for the sending of educational books to prisoners of war. When UNESCO was being organized, the Office of Education participated in the preparatory conferences and, later, in the annual general conferences which decided on general policies and the work to be carried out by the two institutions. After Switzerland joined UNESCO, I was named by my government President of the Swiss Commission of UNESCO and headed the Swiss delegation to the conferences at Bayreuth, Paris, and Florence. UNESCO sent me as a representative to the meetings at Sèvre and Rio de Janeiro, and entrusted me with the editing of the pamphlet *The Right to Education;* I also held for several months the interim post of Assistant Director General in charge of the Department of Education. When M. Torrès-Bodet offered me this post for a longer period, he put me in a somewhat embarrassing position; actually, it did not take me long to decide between the international tasks and the appeal of my uncompleted research: I accepted the offered responsibility, but for only a short time. [In 1950] I accepted, however, membership on the Executive Council of UNESCO, having been elected to it by the general conference at Florence.

While on the subject of international relations, I might mention that in 1946 I had the pleasure of receiving an honorary degree from the Sorbonne; I had been given the same honor by Harvard in 1936 during the unforgettable ceremonies celebrating the tricentenary of that great university. In 1949 I received the honorary doctorate of the University of Brussels and, that same year, the title of Professor, *honoris causa,* of the University of Brazil at Rio de Janeiro. Nor, while writing in this vein, do I wish to fail to mention the pleasure I felt on becoming a member of the New York Academy of Sciences.

But postwar social activities did not cause me to neglect my work. On the contrary, I have gone on a little faster for fear I might not finish in time if the world situation should again become troubled. That explains my many publications. This increase in output, however, does not imply hasty improvisation; I have been working on every one of these publications for a long time.[18]

[18] I have often been asked where I found the time for so much writing in addition to my university work and international duties. I owe it first to the unusual quality of the men and, especially, of the women who have collaborated with me, and who have helped me much more than I can demonstrate here. After years spent in questioning children all by myself, with only small groups of students, latterly I have been helped by teams of assistants and colleagues who did not confine themselves to collecting facts, but took an increasingly active part in conducting this research. And then, too, I owe it to a particular bent of my character. Fundamentally I am a worrier whom only work can relieve. It is true I am sociable and like to teach or to take part in meetings of all kinds, but I feel a compelling need for solitude and contact with nature. After mornings spent with others, I begin each afternoon with a walk during which I quietly collect my thoughts and coordinate them, after which I return to the desk at my home in the country. As soon as vacation time comes, I withdraw to the mountains in the wild regions of the Valais and write for weeks on end on improvised tables and after pleasant walks. It is this dissociation between myself as a social being and as a "man of nature" (in whom Dionysian excitement ends in intellectual

First of all, with the help of B. Inhelder, I was able to carry out about thirty experiments on the development of spatial relations between the ages of two and three, and eleven and twelve,[19] a problem all the more complex because of the constant mutual interference of factors of perception and action. On the other hand, study of intellectual operations as the only reversible mental mechanisms (as opposed to perception, motor performance, etc., which are one-directional) led us to the investigation of the reactions of young children to an irreversible physical phenomena, such as that of mixture or chance.[20] I also finished a study on the genesis of probability with B. Inhelder, which was extended to include the wider problem of induction.

Secondly, I was at last in a position to realize my old plan of writing a genetic epistemology.[21] At the death of Claparède I had given up the course in history of scientific thought to take over experimental psychology. Since I had enough experimental data on the psychological processes underlying logico-mathematical and physical operations, it seemed the right time to write the synthesis I had been dreaming about from the beginning of my studies. Instead of devoting

activity) which has enabled me to surmount a permanent fund of anxiety and transform it into a need for working.

[19] Piaget and Inhelder, *La représentation de l'espace chez l'enfant* (1948); Piaget, Szeminska, and Inhelder, *La géométrie spontanée chez l'enfant* (1948).

[20] *La genèse de l'idée de hasard chez l'enfant* (1951).

[21] *Introduction à l'épistémologie génétique*. I. *La pensée mathématique*, II. *La pensée physique*, III. *La pensée biologique, la pensée psychologique et la pensée sociologique* (1949–1950).

five years to child psychology, as I had anticipated in
1921, I had spent about thirty on it; it was exciting
work and I do not in the least regret it. But now was
the time to conclude it, and that is what I attempted
in this general study. It is basically an analysis of the
mechanism of learning, not statically, but from the
point of view of growth and development.

Lastly, the Colin publishers asked me to write a
Traité de logique[22] with the twofold aim of presenting concisely the operative methods of logistics (or
modern algebraic logic) and of developing my own
ideas on this subject. I hesitated at first since I am not
a logician by profession. But then I was tempted by
the desire to construct a schematic outline of logistics
which would correspond, on the one hand, to the steps
in the formation of operations (concrete operations of
class and relationship—formal operation, or the logic
of propositions), and, on the other hand, to the kinds
of structures the fundamental psychological importance of which I had previously discovered. Since then
I have written a shorter work, not yet published,*
which deals with structures-of-the-whole (groups,
lattices, and groupings) which can be defined by
means of three propositions (the logic of the 256
ternary operations).

---

[22] *Traité de logique, esquisse d'une logistique opératoire*
(1949).

* Since this autobiography was first published, Dr. Piaget
has completed this work on groups and lattices: J. Piaget, *Essai
sur les transformations des opérations logiques. Les 256 opérations ternaires de la logique bivalente des propositions* (Paris:
Presses Universitaires de France, 1952).

Conclusion

My one idea, developed under various aspects in (alas!) twenty-two volumes, has been that intellectual operations proceed in terms of structures-of-the-whole. These structures denote the kinds of equilibrium toward which evolution in its entirety is striving; at once organic, psychological, and social, their roots reach down as far as biological morphogenesis itself.

This idea is doubtless more widespread than is generally assumed; however, it had never been satisfactorily demonstrated. After more than thirty years' work on the higher aspects of that evolution, I should like one day to go back to the more primitive mechanisms; this is one reason why I am interested in infantile perceptions. The reversibility characteristic of the operations of logical intelligence is not acquired *en bloc,* but is prepared in the course of a series of successive stages: elementary rhythms, more and more complex regulations (semireversible structures), and, ultimately, reversible operative structures. Now this law of evolution, which dominates all mental development, corresponds no doubt to certain laws of structuration of the nervous system which it would be interesting to try to formulate in regard to qualitative mathematical structures (groups, lattices, etc.).[23] As to Gestalt structures, they constitute only one par-

[23] Piaget, Le problème neurologique de l'interiorisation des actions en opérations réversibles, *Arch. de Psychol.* (1949), 32, 241–258.

ticular type among possible structures, and these belong to regulations rather than to (reversible) operations. I hope to be able someday to demonstrate
relationships between mental structures and stages of
nervous development, and thus to arrive at that general theory of structures to which my earlier studies
constitute merely an introduction.

Addendum

Since the writing of his autobiography, Piaget's continued analysis of intellectual development has had
an increasingly forceful impact on the fields of education and developmental psychology. An international
Center for Genetic Epistemology was established by
Piaget at the University of Geneva in 1956. Based
upon interdisciplinary symposia held at the center, a
monograph series (*Studies in Genetic Epistemology*)
has appeared focusing on many contemporary issues
of cognitive development.

Piaget has continued to produce and generate
numerous theoretical and research publications and
books, each dealing with a particular aspect of intellectual achievement (e.g., the growth of logical
thinking, the development of mental images, biological
factors as they relate to cognitive processes, and
memory processes of children). He is currently involved with research pertaining to the development of
the child's conception of causality, as he mentions in
the dialogue.

Remarkably, since the publication of this autobiography in 1952, Piaget's importance and influence

among American psychologists have finally grown to the point where he was described, upon being awarded the 1969 Distinguished Scientific Contribution Award by the American Psychological Association, as follows:

> To Jean Piaget, for his revolutionary perspective on the nature of human knowledge and biological intelligence. Starting as a biologist interested in the history of scientific thinking, he has approached heretofore exclusive philosophical questions in a resolutely empirical fashion and created epistemology as a science, separate from philosophy, but interrelated with all human sciences. Almost as a by-product of this his chief work he has amassed during half a century ingenious observations and controlled data on human thinking which represent a unique and lasting monument in the psychological literature. Having been known and honored all over the world since his early writings, he becomes the first European to receive the APA Distinguished Scientific Contribution Award. Our organization thereby recognizes the seminal influence which this Swiss scientist exerts on all scholars concerned with human knowing and its development.

Following is a list of Jean Piaget's major works:

Scientific Publications

1907
Un moineau albinos. *Rameau de Sapin* (Neuchâtel), 41 (9), 36.

1911
Mollusques recueillis dans la région supérieure du Val d'Hérens. *Rameau de Sapin* (Neuchâtel), 45, 30–32, 40, 46–47.
Les limnées des lacs de Neuchâtel, Morat et des environs (note sur 3 variétés nouvelles de mollusques suisses). *Journal de Conchyliologie.*

1912

Supplément au catalogue des mollusques du Canton de Neuchâtel. *Bulletin de la Société neuchâteloise des Sciences Naturelles*, 39, 74–89.

Les limnées des lacs de Neuchâtel, Bienne, Morat et des environs. *Journal de Conchyliologie*.

Note sur trois variétés nouvelles de mollusques suisses. *Journal de Conchyliologie*.

Quelques mollusques de Colombie. *Mémoires de la Société neuchâteloise des Sciences Naturelles*, 5.

With M. ROMY. Les mollusques du lac de Saint-Blaise. *Bulletin de la Société neuchâteloise de Géographie*.

1913

Premières recherches sur les mollusques profonds du lac de Neuchâtel. *Bulletin de la Société neuchâteloise des Sciences Naturelles*, 40, 148–171.

Les mollusques sublittoraux du Léman recueillis par M. le Pr Yung. *Zoologischer Anzeiger* (Leipzig), 42, 615–624.

Les récents dragages malacologiques de M. le Pr Yung dans le lac Léman. *Journal de Conchyliologie*, 60, 205–232.

Nouveaux dragages malacologiques de M. le Pr Yung dans la faune profonde du Léman. *Zoologischer Anzeiger* (Leipzig), 42, 216–225.

Malacologie alpestre. *Revue suisse de Zoologie*, 21, 439–576.

Malacologie de Duingt et des environs. *Revue savoisienne* (Annecy), 54, 69–85, 166–180, 234–242.

Malacologie du Vully. *Mémoires de la Société fribourgeoise des Sciences Naturelles*, Série Zoologie, Vol. I, fasc. 3, 48 pages.

1914

Un mollusque arctique habitant les Alpes suisses. *Feuille des Jeunes Naturalistes* (Paris), 44, 5–6.

Un mollusque nouveau pour la faune argovienne. *Feuille des Jeunes Naturalistes* (Paris), 44, 148.

Contribution à la malacologie terrestre et fluviatile de la Bretagne. *Bulletin de la Société neuchâteloise des Sciences Naturelles*, 41, 32–83.

Étude zoogéographique de quelques dépôts coquilliers quaternaires du Seeland et des environs. *Mitteilungen der naturforschenden Gesellschaft* (Bern), 105–106.

L'espèce mendelienne a-t-elle une valeur absolue? *Zoologischer Anzeiger* (Leipzig), 44, 328–331.

Note sur la Biologie des Limnées abyssales. *Internationale Revue der Hydrologie und Hydrographie*, Supplément biologique, 6, 1–15.

1915

Révision de quelques mollusques glaciaires du musée d'histoire naturelle de Berne. *Mitteilungen der naturforschenden Gesellschaft* (Bern), 218–277.

1916

La mission de l'idée. Lausanne: Édition "La Concorde."

Nouvelles recherches sur les mollusques du Val Ferret et des environs immédiats. *Bulletin de la Société La Murithienne* (Sion) 29, 22–73. Also published at Sion: F. Aymon.

1917

Note sur quelques mollusques de la vallée du Doubs. *Mémoires de la Société d'Émulation du Doubs* (Montbéliard), 1–14.

1918

Recherche. Lausanne: Édition "La Concorde."

1920

Corrélation entre la répartition verticale des mollusques du Valais et les indices de variations spécifiques. *Revue suisse de Zoologie,* 28 (7), 125–133.

Introduction à la malacologie valaisanne. *Bulletin de la Société La Murithienne* (Sion), 40, 86–186.

La psychanalyse et ses rapports avec la psychologie de l'enfant. *Bulletin de la Société Alfred Binet,* 20 (131, 132, 133), 18–34, 41–58.

1921

Introduction à la malacologie valaisanne. (Doctoral dissertation.) Sion: F. Aymon.

Essai sur quelques aspects du développement de la notion de partie chez l'enfant. *Journal de Psychologie,* 18, 449–480.

1922

Essai sur la multiplication logique et les débuts de la pensée formelle chez l'enfant. *Journal de Psychologie,* 19, 222–261.

Pour l'étude des explications d'enfants. *L'Éducateur,* 3, 33–39.

1923

Le langage et la pensée chez l'enfant. Neuchâtel & Paris:
Delachaux & Niestlé. (2nd ed. 1931; 3rd ed. 1947; 4th ed.
1956; 5th ed. 1962.)
Translations:
  The Language and the Thought of the Child. (Trans. by
    M. Gabain.) London: Kegan Paul, 1926. (2nd ed., Lon-
    don: Routledge and Kegan Paul, 1948; 3rd ed. 1959.)
  The Language and Thought of the Child. (Trans. by
    M. Gabain.) New York: Meridian Books, 1955.
  The Language and the Thought of the Child. (Ed. by
    Shipley & Thorne.) New York: Classics in Psychology,
    Philosophical Library, 1961.
  El lenguaje y el pensamiento en el niño. (Trans. by
    D. Barñes.) Madrid: Ediciones de "La Lectura."
  Il linguaggio e il pensiero del fanciullo. (Trans. by C. Mu-
    satti-Rapuzzi.) Firenze: Editrice Universitaria, 1955. (2nd
    ed. 1962.)
  A linguagem e o pensamento da criança. (Trans. by M. Cam-
    pos.) Rio de Janeiro: Fundo de Cultura.
  Coçukta del ve düsünnie. Istambul: Devle Basimevi.
La psychologie et les valeurs religieuses. Geneva: Labor.
Une forme verbale de la comparaison chez l'enfant. *Archives de
  Psychologie, 18, 141–172.*
With P. Rossello. Note sur les types de description d'images
  chez l'enfant. *Archives de Psychologie, 18, 208–234.*
La pensée symbolique et la pensée de l'enfant. *Archives de
  Psychologie, 18, 273–304.*

1924

Le jugement et le raisonnement chez l'enfant. Neuchâtel &
Paris: Delachaux & Niestlé. (2nd ed. 1930; 3rd ed. 1947;
4th ed. 1948; 5th ed. 1963.)
Translations:
  Judgment and Reasoning in the Child. New York: Harcourt
    & Brace, 1926. (2nd ed. 1938.)
  Sadi rozumowanie u dziecka. (Trans. by Jadwiga Pini-
    Suchodolska.) Lwow: Ksiaznica Atlas, 1939.
  Coçukta hüküm ve himiakeve. Istambul: Devle Basimevi,
    1939.

Giudizio e ragionamento nel bambino. (Trans. by Elena Nunberg-Almansi.) Firenze: La Nuova Italia, 1958.

El juicio y el razonamiento en el niño. (Trans. by D. Barñes.) Madrid: Ediciones de "La Lectura."

Les traits principaux de la logique de l'enfant. *Journal de Psychologie,* 21, 48–101.

L'expérience humaine et la causalité physique de L. Brunschwieg. *Journal de Psychologie,* 21, 586–607.

1925

Psychologie et critique de la connaissance. *Archives de Psychologie,* 19, 193–210.

With MLLE MARGAIRAZ. La structure des récits et l'interprétation des images de Dawid chez l'enfant. *Archives de Psychologie,* 19, 211–239.

Quelques explications d'enfants relatives à l'origine des astres. *Journal de Psychologie,* 22, 677–702.

De quelques formes primitives de causalité chez l'enfant. *L'Année psychologique,* 26, 31–71.

Le réalisme nominal chez l'enfant. *Revue philosophique,* 54, 188–234.

La représentation du monde de l'enfant. *Revue de Théologie et de Philosophie* (Lausanne), 13, 191–214.

Malacologie valaisanne. *Bulletin de la Société La Murithienne* (Sion), 42, 82–112.

With H. KRAFFT. La notion de l'ordre des événements et le test des images en désordre. *Archives de Psychologie,* 19, 306–349.

1926

La représentation du monde chez l'enfant. Paris: Alcan. (2nd ed. 1938; new ed. Paris: P. U. F., 1947.)

Translations:

The Child's Conception of the World. New York: Harcourt & Brace, 1929. (Reprint: New Jersey: Littlefield-Adams, 1960.)

Jak sobie dziecko swiat przedstawia? (Trans. by Marja Ziembinska.) Lwow: Ksiaznica Atlas, 1933.

La representacion del mundo en el niño. (Trans. by Vicente Valla Angles.) Madrid: Espasa Calpe, 1934.

Rinskô jidô shinrigaku. (Vol. 1) (Trans. by Shigeru Otomo.) Tokyo: Hakuslisha, 1954.

Jidô no sekaikan. (Vol. 2) Tokyo: Dôbun, 1955.

La rappresentazione del mondo nel fanciullo. (Trans. by Maria Villaroel with preface by C. Musatti.) Torino: Einaudi, 1955.

El nacimento de la inteligenzia en el niño. *Revista de Pédagogia* (Madrid), 5, 529–536.

Chap. Psychology. In, Review of the philosophical work in France and in French-speaking countries. *The Monist* (Chicago), 36, 430–455.

1927

La causalité physique chez l'enfant. Paris: Alcan.

Translations:

    The Child's Conception of Physical Causality. Totowa, N.J.: Littlefield, Adams, Patterson, 1960.

    La causalidad fisica del niño. (Trans. by Juan Comas.) Madrid: Espasa Calpe.

La première année de l'enfant. *The British Journal of Psychology*, 18, 97–120.

L'explication de l'ombre chez l'enfant. *Journal de Psychologie*, 24, 230–242.

1928

With J. DE LA HARPE. *Deux types d'attitudes religieuses. Immanence et transcendance*. Geneva: Labor.

La causalité chez l'enfant. *The British Journal of Psychology*, 18, 276–301.

La règle morale chez l'enfant. *Stiftung Lucerna*, 2, 32–45.

Les trois systèmes de la pensée de l'enfant. *Bulletin de la Société française de Philosophie*, 28, 97–138.

Psycho-pédagogie et mentalité enfantine. *Journal de Psychologie*, 25, 31–60.

Logique génétique et sociologie. *Revue philosophique*, 167–205.

Un problème d'hérédité chez la Limnée des étangs. Appel aux macologistes et aux amateurs en onchyliologie. *Bulletin de la Société zoologique de France*, 53, 13–18.

Psychology. In E. L. Schaub (Ed.), *Philosophy Today*. Chicago and London. Pp. 263–288.

1929

L'adaptation de la Limnaea stagnalis aux milieux lacustres de la Suisse romande. *Revue suisse de Zoologie*, 36, 3–6.

Les races lacustres de la Limnaea stagnalis. Recherches sur les rapports de l'adaptation héréditaire avec le milieu. *Bulletin biologique de la France et de la Belgique* (Paris), 63, 424–455.

Les deux directions de la pensée scientifique. Compte rendu des séances de la Société de Physique et d'Histoire naturelle de Genève. *Archives des Sciences physiques et naturelles*, 11, 145–162.

1930

Immanentisme et foi religieuse. Geneva: Robert.

Catalogue des invertébrés de la Suisse de G. Mermod. (Collab. au fasc. 18.) Geneva: Albert Kundig.

Les procédés de l'éducation morale. *Cinquième Congrès International d'Éducation morale.* Paris: Alcan. Pp. 182–219.

Le développement de l'esprit de solidarité chez l'enfant. *Troisième cours pour le personnel enseignant:* Comment faire connaître la Société des Nations et développer l'esprit de coopération internationale. *Compte rendu des conférences données du 28 juillet au 2 août 1930.* Geneva: B. I. E. No. 8, pp. 52–55.

La notion de justice chez l'enfant. *Troisième cours pour le personnel enseignant. Ibid.,* pp. 55–57.

1931

Le développement intellectuel chez les jeunes enfants. *Mind,* 40, 137–160.

Retrospective and Prospective Analysis in Child Psychology. *The British Journal of Educational Psychology,* 1, 130–139.

Children's Philosophies. In Murchison (Ed.), *A Handbook of Child Psychology.* Worcester, Mass., pp. 377–391.

Introduction psychologique à l'éducation internationale. *Quatrième cours pour le personnel enseignant:* Comment faire connaître la Société des Nations et développer l'esprit de coopération internationale. *Compte rendu des conférences données du 3 au 8 août 1931.* Geneva: B. I. E. No. 9, pp. 56–68.

L'esprit de solidarité chez l'enfant et la collaboration internationale. *Bulletin de l'enseignement de la Société des Nations,* Geneva, 2, 11–27.

1932

Le jugement moral chez l'enfant. Paris: Alcan. (New ed., Paris: P. U. F., 1957.)

Translations:

The Moral Judgment of the Child. (Trans. by Marjorie Gabain.) New York:' Harcourt. (2nd ed. Glencoe, Ill.: Free Press, 1948.)

El juicio moral en el niño. (Trans. by Juan Comas.) Madrid: Beltran, 1935.

Das moralische Urteil beim Kinde. (Trans. by L. Goldmann.) Zurich: Rascher Verlag, 1954.

Jidô Dôtoku Haudau no Hattatsu. (Trans. by Shigeru Otomo.) Tokyo: Dôbun Shoin.

Sad moralny u dziecka. Varsovie: Panstwowe Wydawnictwo Naukowe, in press.

Social Evolution and the New Education. (Vol. 8.) London: New Education Fellowship.

Les difficultés psychologiques de l'éducation internationale. *Cinquième cours pour le personnel enseignant.* Comment faire connaître la Société des Nations et développer l'esprit de coopération internationale. *Compte rendu des conférences données du 25 au 30 juillet 1932.* Geneva: B. I. E. No. 8, pp. 57–76.

1933

Psychologie de l'enfant et enseignement de l'histoire. *Bulletin trim. de la Conférence internationale pour l'enseignement de l'histoire,* Paris, 2.

Le Bureau International d'Éducation en 1931–1932. Rapport du directeur. *Annuaire International de l'Éducation et de l'Enseignement 1933.* Geneva: B. I. E. No. 27, pp. 303–333.

L'individualité en histoire. L'individu et la formation de la raison. In, *L'individualité, 3me semaine internationale de Synthèse.* Fondation Pour la Science. Centre International de Synthèse. Paris: Alcan, pp. 67–121.

La psychanalyse et le développement intellectuel. *Revue française de psychanalyse,* 6, 404–408.

1934

Remarques psychologiques sur le self-government. *Le self-government à l'école.* Geneva: B. I. E. No. 38, pp. 89–108.

Le Bureau International d'Éducation en 1932–1933. Rapport du directeur. *Annuaire International de l'Éducation et de l'Enseignement 1934.* Geneva: B. I. E. No. 35, pp. 443–470.

1935

Les théories de l'imitation. *Cahiers de pédagogie expérimentale et de psychologie de l'enfant.* Geneva, 1935, No. 6.

Preface to A. Rey: *L'intelligence pratique chez l'enfant.* Paris: Alcan, pp. VII–XII.

Le Bureau International d'Éducation en 1933–1934. Rapport du directeur. *Annuaire International de l'Éducation et de l'Enseignement 1935.* Geneva: B. I. E. No. 43, pp. 403–426.

Remarques psychologiques sur le travail par équipes. *Le travail par équipes à l'école.* Geneva: B. I. E., pp. 179–196.

La naissance de l'intelligence chez le petit enfant. *Revue de pédagogie,* ULB (Bruxelles), 11, 56–83.

1936

La naissance de l'intelligence chez l'enfant. Neuchâtel & Paris: Delachaux & Niestlé. (2nd ed. 1948; 3rd ed. 1959; 4th ed. 1963.)

Translations:

The Origins of Intelligence in Children. (Trans. by M. Cook.) New York: International Universities Press. (2nd ed. New York: Norton, 1963.)

The Origin of Intelligence in the Child. (Trans. by M. Cook.) London: Routledge and Kegan Paul, 1953.

The Origin of Intelligence in Children. (Trans. by M. Cook.) London: Bailey Bros. and Swinfen.

Navodziny inteligencji u dziecka. Varsovie: Panstwowe Wydawnictwo Naukowe, in press.

L'enseignement des langues vivantes. *Bulletin de l'enseignement de la Société des Nations,* Geneva, 3, 61–66.

Le Bureau International d'Éducation en 1934–1935. Rapport du directeur. *Annuaire International de l'Éducation et de l'Enseignement 1936.* Geneva: B. I. E. No. 50, pp. 429–450.

1937

La construction du réel chez l'enfant. Neuchâtel & Paris: Delachaux & Niestlé. (2nd ed. 1950; 3rd ed. 1963.)

Translations:

The Construction of Reality in the Child. (Trans. by M. Cook.) New York: Basic Books, 1954.

The Child's Construction of Reality. (Trans. by M. Cook.) London: Routledge and Kegan Paul, 1955.

Principal Factors Determining Intellectual Evolution from Childhood to Adult Life. *Harvard Tercentenary Celebration, 1936.* Cambridge, Mass.: Harvard University Press.

Les relations d'égalité résultant de l'addition et de la soustraction logiques constituent-elles un groupe? *L'enseignement mathématique* (Geneva), 1–2, 99–108.

La philosophie de Gustave Juvet. *A la mémoire de Gustave Juvet,* Lausanne, 37–52.

Remarques psychologiques sur les relations entre la classe logique et le nombre et sur les rapports d'inclusion. *Recueil de travaux de l'Université de Lausanne. Publ. à l'occasion du IVᵉ centenaire de la fondation de l'Université.* Lausanne, pp. 59–85.

L'enseignement de la Psychologie. *Documents officiels sur l'enseignement de la Psychologie dans la préparation des maîtres primaires et secondaires.* Geneva: B. I. E., pp. 5–28.

Le Bureau International d'Éducation en 1935–1936. Rapport du directeur. *Annuaire International de l'Éducation et de l'Enseignement 1937.* Geneva: B. I. E. No. 56, pp. 405–420.

1938

Le Bureau International d'Éducation en 1937–1938. *Rapport du directeur à la neuvième réunion du Conseil.* Geneva: B. I. E.

Le problème de l'intelligence et de l'habitude: Réflexe conditionné, "Gestalt" ou assimilation. *XIᵉ Congrès international de Psychologie, Paris 1937.* Paris, pp. 170–183.

La réversibilité des opérations et l'importance de la notion de "groupe" pour la psychologie de la pensée. *XIᵉ Congrès international de Psychologie, Paris 1937.* Paris, pp. 433–435.

1939

Le Bureau International d'Éducation en 1938–1939. *Rapport du directeur à la dixième réunion du Conseil.* Geneva: B. I. E.

Les méthodes nouvelles, leurs bases psychologiques. *Encyclopédie Française,* 15(26), 4–16.

Méthodes fondées sur les mecanismes individuels de la pensée. *Encyclopédie Française,* 15(28), 1–10.

Méthodes fondées sur la vie sociale de l'enfant. *Encyclopédie Française*, 15(28), 10–13.

With A. SZEMINSKA. Quelques expériences sur la conservation des quantités continues chez l'enfant. *Journal de Psychologie*, 36, 36–64.

La construction psychologique du nombre entier. Compte rendu des séances de la Société de Physique et d'Histoire naturelle de Genève. *Archives des sciences physiques et naturelles*, 92–95.

1940

Le Bureau International d'Éducation en 1939–1940. Rapport du directeur. Geneva: B. I. E.

Essai sur la théorie des valeurs qualitatives en sociologie statique. *Publications de la Faculté des Sciences économiques et sociales de l'Université de Genève*, 3, 31–79.

Le groupement additif des relations transitives asymétriques. Mélanges Arnold Reymond. *Revue de Théologie et de Philosophie* (Lausanne), 146–152.

1941

With A. SZEMINSKA. *La genèse du nombre chez l'enfant*. Neuchâtel & Paris: Delachaux & Niestlé. (2nd ed. 1950; 3rd ed. 1964.)

Translations:

> *The Child's Conception of Number*. (*Trans. by C. Gattegno & F. M. Hodgson*.) London: Routledge and Kegan Paul, 1952. (2nd ed. 1961; 3rd ed. 1965.)
>
> *Die Entwicklung des Zahlbegriffes beim Kind*. Stuttgart: Klett-Verlag, 1965.
>
> *Kazu no hattatsu shingrigaten*. (Trans. by Hiraku Tôyama *et al.*) Tokyo: Kokudosha, 1962.

With B. INHELDER. *Le développement des quantités chez l'enfant. Conservation et atomisme*. Neuchâtel & Paris: Delachaux & Niestlé, 1941.

Le développement des quantités physiques chez l'enfant. Conservation et atomisme. 2nd ed., augmentée, *ibid.*, 1962.

Translation:

> *Ryo no hatatsu shinrigaku*. Tokyo, 1965.

Le Bureau International d'Éducation en 1940–1941. Rapport du directeur. Geneva: B. I. E.

Esprit et réalité. *Annuaire de la Société suisse de Philosophie,*
1, 40–47.

La psychologie d'Édouard Claparède. *Archives de Psychologie,*
28, 193–213.

Le mécanisme du développement mental et les lois du groupement des opérations. Esquisse de l'une théorie opératoire de
l'intelligence. *Archives de Psychologie,* 28, 215–285.

Quelques observations sur le développement psychologique de
la notion de temps. Compte rendu des séances de la Société
de Physique et d'Histoire naturelle de Genève. *Archives des
sciences physiques et naturelles,* 21–24.

L'axiomatique des opérations constitutives du temps. *Archives
des sciences physiques et naturelles,* 24–28.

Le rôle de la tautologie dans la composition additive des classes
et des ensembles. *Archives des sciences physiques et naturelles,* 102–107.

Le groupement additif des classes. *Archives des sciences physiques et naturelles,* 107–112.

Le groupement additif des relations asymétriques (sériation
qualitative) et ses rapports avec le groupement additif des
classes. *Archives des sciences physiques et naturelles,* 117–
122.

Sur les rapports entre les groupements additifs des classes et
des relations asymétriques et le groupe additif des nombres
entiers. *Archives des sciences physiques et naturelles,* 122–
126.

Les groupements de la classification complète et de l'addition
des relations symétriques. *Archives des sciences physiques et
naturelles,* 149–154.

Les groupements de la multiplication biunivoque des classes et
de celle des relations. *Archives des sciences physiques et
naturelles,* 154–159.

Les groupements de la multiplication co-univoque des classes et
des relations. *Archives des sciences physiques et naturelles,*
192–197.

La fonction régulatrice du groupement dans le développement
mental: Esquisse d'une théorie opératoire de l'intelligence.
Archives des sciences physiques et naturelles, 198–203.

1942

*Classes, relations et nombres. Essai sur les groupements de la
logistique et sur la réversibilité de la pensée.* Paris: Vrin.

Le Bureau International d'Éducation en 1941–1942. Rapport du directeur. Geneva: B. I. E.

Les trois structures fondamentales de la vie psychique: Rythme, régulation et groupement. *Revue suisse de Psychologie*, 1, 9–21.

Une expérience sur le développement de la notion du temps. *Revue suisse de Psychologie*, 1, 179–185.

With M. LAMBERCIER, E. BOESCH, & B. v. ALBERTINI. Introduction à l'étude des perceptions chez l'enfant et analyse d'une illusion relative à la perception visuelle de cercles concentriques (Delbœuf). *Archives de Psychologie*, 29, 1–107.

La notion de régulation dans l'étude des illusions perceptives. Compte rendu des séances de la Société de Physique et d'Histoire naturelle de Genève. *Archives des sciences physiques et naturelles*, 72–74.

Psychologie et Pédagogie genevoises. *Suisse Contemporaine*, 427–431.

Intellectual Evolution. In, *Science and Man*. New York: Harcourt and Brace, pp. 409–422.

1943

Preface to B. Inhelder: *Le diagnostic du raisonnement chez les débiles mentaux*. Neuchâtel & Paris: Delachaux & Niestlé. Pp. 1–4. (2nd ed. 1963, pp. 1–3.)

Le développement mental de l'enfant. *Juventus Helvetica. Notre jeune génération*. Zurich: Litteraria, pp. 19–76.

Translation:

Die geistige Entwicklung des Kindes. (Trans. by B. Inhelder.) *Juventus Helvetica. Unsere junge Generation*. Zurich: M. S. Metz, 1944. Pp. 31–92.

With M. LAMBERCIER. La comparaison visuelle des hauteurs à distances variables dans le plan frontoparallèle. *Archives de Psychologie*, 29, 173–253.

With M. LAMBERCIER. Le problème de la comparaison visuelle en profondeur et l'erreur systématique de l'étalon. *Archives de Psychologie*, 29, 255–308.

La perception chez les vertébrés supérieurs et chez le jeune enfant. *Revue suisse de Zoologie*, 50, 225–232.

Interprétation probabiliste de la loi de Weber et de celle des centrations relatives. Compte rendu des séances de la Société de Physique et d'Histoire naturelle de Genève. *Archives des sciences physiques et naturelles*, 200–204.

1944

Les relations entre la morale et le droit. In, *Mélanges d'études économiques et sociales offerts à William E. Rappard*. Publication de la Faculté des Sciences économiques et sociales de l'Université de Genève, 8, 19–54.

L'organisation et l'esprit de la psychologie à Genève. *Revue suisse de Psychologie*, 3, 97–104.

With B. ALBERTINI & M. ROSSI. Essai d'interprétation probabiliste de la loi de Weber et de celle des centrations relatives. *Archives de Psychologie*, 30, 95–138.

With M. LAMBERCIER. Essai sur un effet d'Einstellung survenant au cours de perceptions visuelles successives (effet Usnadze). *Archives de Psychologie*, 30, 139–196.

1945

With B. INHELDER. Expériences sur la construction projective de la ligne droite chez l'enfant de 2 à 8 ans. *Cahiers de Pédagogie expérimentale et de Psychologie de l'enfant*, 2, 1–17.

Preface to M. Rambert: *La vie affective et morale de l'enfant*. Neuchâtel & Paris: Delachaux & Niestlé. Pp. 3–4.

Hommage à C. G. Jung. *Revue suisse de Psychologie*, 4, 160–171.

Les opérations logiques et la vie sociale. In, Publ. Fac. Sc. Econ. et sociales de l'Union de Genève, 9.

1946

La formation du symbole chez l'enfant. Neuchâtel & Paris: Delachaux & Niestlé. (2nd ed. 1959; 3rd ed. 1964.)

Translations:

Play, Dreams, Imitation in Childhood. (Trans. by C. Gattegno & F. M. Hodgson.) New York: Norton, 1951.

Play, Dreams and Imitation in Childhood. London: Heinemann, 1951.

Le développement de la notion de temps chez l'enfant. Paris: P. U. F.

Translation:

Die Bildung des Zeitbegriffs beim Kinde. (Trans. by G. Meili-Dworetski.) Zurich: Rascher Verlag, 1955.

Les notions de mouvement et de vitesse chez l'enfant. Paris: P. U. F.

With F. GONSETH. Groupement, groupes et lattices. *Archives de Psychologie,* 31, 65–73.

With M. LAMBERCIER. Transpositions perceptives et transitivité opératoire dans les comparaisons en profondeur. *Archives de Psychologie,* 31, 325–368.

1947

La psychologie de l'intelligence. Paris: A. Colin. (Reedited: 1947, 1949, 1952, 1956, 1961, 1962, 1964, 1965.)

Translations:

Psychologie der Intelligenz. (Trans. by L. Goldmann & Y. Moser.) Zurich: Rascher Verlag, 1958. (Reedition 1966.)

The Psychology of Intelligence. (Trans. by M. Piercey & D. E. Berlyne.) London: Routledge and Kegan Paul, 1950. (Reprint: New Jersey: Littlefield, Adams, Patterson, 1960.)

Intelligensens Psykologi. Stockholm: Natur ochs Kultur, 1951.

Psicologia dell'Intelligenza. (Trans. by Dino Di Giorgi.) Firenze: Editrice Universitaria, 1952.

Psicologia de la Inteligencia. (Trans. by Juan Carlos Faix.) Buenos-Aires, 1956.

Psicologia da inteligência. (Trans. by C. de Alencar.) Rio de Janeiro: Fundo de Cultura, 1958.

E psychologia tes noemosynes. (Trans. by Sp. Rallis.) Athenai, 1958.

Preface to L. Johannot: *Le raisonnement mathématique de l'adolescent.* Neuchâtel & Paris: Delachaux & Niestlé.

Preface to N. Kostyleff: *La réflexologie et les essais d'une psychologie structurale.* Neuchâtel & Paris: Delachaux & Niestlé, pp. 7–10.

Preface to Ed. Claparède: *Psychologie de l'enfant et pédagogie expérimentale.* (Reedition.) Neuchâtel & Paris: Delachaux & Niestlé, pp. 7–31.

Translation:

Ed. Claparède: *Pedagogia sperimentale. I metodi.* Con un studio di J. Piaget sulla Psicologia di Edouard Claparède. (Trans. by B. Garan & G. Petter.) Firenze: Ed. Universitaria, 1956.

Du rapport des Sciences avec la Philosophie. *Synthèse,* 130–150.

With B. INHELDER. Diagnosis of Mental Operations and Theory

of the Intelligence. *American Journal of Mental Deficiency*, 51, 401–406.

Des intuitions topologiques élémentaires à la construction eucli-dienne dans le développement psychologique de l'espace (titre de communication). Compte rendu des séances de la Société de Physique et d'Histoire naturelle de Genève. *Archives des Sciences physiques et naturelles*, 64, 31.

La soustraction des surfaces partielles congruentes à deux sur-faces totales égales. *Miscellanea Psychologica Albert Michotte*. Louvain & Paris: Nauwelaerts & Vrin. Pp. 167–180.

1948

With B. INHELDER. *La représentation de l'espace chez l'enfant*. Paris: P. U. F.

Translation:

    The Child's Conception of Space. (Trans. by Langdon & Lunzer.) London: Routledge and Kegan Paul, 1956.

With B. INHELDER & A. SZEMINSKA. *La géométrie spontanée de l'enfant*. Paris: P. U. F.

Translation:

    The Child's Conception of Geometry. (Trans. by G. A. Lunzer.) London: Routledge and Kegan Paul, 1960.

L'analyse psycho-génétique et l'épistémologie des sciences ex-actes. *Synthèse*, 32–49.

Pierre Janet. *Archives de Psychologie*, 32, 235–237.

1949

Traité de logique. Essai de logistique opératoire. Paris: A. Colin.

La genèse du nombre chez l'enfant. In, *Initiation au calcul* (enfants de 4 à 7 ans) (avec B. Boscher, A. Chatelet). *Cahiers de pédagogie moderne*. Paris: Bourrelier. Pp. 5–28.

Translations:

    Avviamento al calcolo. (Trans. by E. Nunberg Almansi.) Firenze: La Nuova Italia, 1956. Pp. 3–45.

    L'insegnamento della matematica. (Trans. by M. G. Campe-delli.) Firenze: La Nuova Italia, 1960. Pp. 1–35.

    Die Genese der Zahl beim Kinde. (Trans. by Theo Kern.) In, *Rechnenunterricht und Zahlbegriff*. Westermann Taschen-buch (Theorie und Praxis der Schule), 1964, pp. 50–72. (2nd ed. 1965.)

The Right to Education in the Modern World. In, *UNESCO, Freedom and Culture.* New York: Columbia University Press, 1951. Pp. 67–116.

Le groupe des transformations de la logique des propositions bivalentes. Compte rendu des séances de la Société de Physique et d'Histoire naturelle de Genève. *Archives des Sciences physiques et naturelles,* 154, 179–182.

Le problème neurologique de l'intériorisation des actions en opérations réversibles. *Archives de Psychologie,* 32, 241–258.

With H. Würsten & L. Johannot. Les illusions relatives aux angles et à la longueur de leurs côtés. *Archives de Psychologie,* 32, 281–307.

Remarques psychologiques sur l'enseignement élémentaire des Sciences naturelles. In, *L'initiation aux Sciences naturelles à l'école primaire.* Geneva: UNESCO-B.I.E., 110, 35–45.

1950

Introduction à l'épistémologie génétique, tome I: *La pensée mathématique.* Paris: P. U. F.

Introduction à l'épistémologie génétique, tome II: *La pensée physique,* Paris: P. U. F.

Introduction à l'épistémologie génétique, tome III: *La pensée biologique, la pensée psychologique et la pensée sociologique.* Paris: P. U. F.

Schémas mathématiques, biologiques et physiques. *Études de Philosophie des Sciences, en hommage à Ferdinand Gonseth, à l'occasion de son 60ᵉ anniversaire.* Neuchâtel: Éd. du Griffon. Pp. 143–146.

La psychologie de l'enfant, de 1946 à 1948. In, *Institut International de Philosophie,* XIV: *Psychologie, Phénoménologie et Existentialisme.* Paris: Hermann. Pp. 89–111.

With B. von Albertini. L'illusion de Müller-Lyer. *Archives de Psychologie,* 33, 1–48.

Sur la logique des propositions. Compte rendu des séances de la Société de Physique et d'Histoire naturelle de Genève. *Archives des Sciences physiques et naturelles,* 155, 159–161.

Épistémologie génétique et méthodologie dialectique. *Dialectica,* 4, 287–295.

Perception et intelligence. *Bulletin du groupe d'études de psychologie de l'Université de Paris,* 4, 1–2, 25–34.

With B. Inhelder. Le rôle des opérations dans le développement de l'intelligence. *Proceedings and Papers of the XIIth*

International Congress of Psychology, Edinburgh 1948. Edinburgh: Oliver and Boyd. Pp. 102–103.

Droits à l'éducation dans le monde actuel. Les Droits de l'esprit. In, *Collection Droits de l'Homme.* Paris: UNESCO. Pp. 21–72.

Une expérience sur la psychologie du hasard chez l'enfant: Le tirage au sort des couples. *Acta psychologica,* 7, 323–336.

L'utilité de la logistique en psychologie. *L'année psychologique,* 50, 27–38.

1951

With B. INHELDER. *La genèse de l'idée de hasard chez l'enfant.* Paris: P. U. F.

Preface to H. Aebli: *Didactique psychologique. Application à la didactique de la psychologie de Jean Piaget.* Neuchâtel & Paris: Delachaux & Niestlé. Pp. V–VI.

With B. INHELDER. Die Psychologie der frühen Kindheit. In D. Katz (Ed.), *Handbuch der Psychologie.* Bâle. Pp. 232–271. (2nd ed. 1959–60.)

Translations:

Spanish: Madrid: Morata, 1954. Pp. 231–267.

Swedish: Stockholm: Svenska Boksörlaget Bonnia, 1955. Pp. 261–294.

Italian: Torino: Boringhieri, 1960. Pp. 272–309.

Intelligenza. *Enciclopedia medica italiana,* 617–622.

With M. LAMBERCIER. La comparaison des grandeurs projectives chez l'enfant et chez l'adulte. *Archives de Psychologie,* 33, 81–130.

With M. LAMBERCIER. La perception d'un carré animé d'un mouvement de circumduction (effet Auersperg et Buhrmester). *Archives de Psychologie,* 33, 131–195.

Pensée égocentrique et pensée sociocentrique. *Cahiers internationaux de sociologie,* 10, 34–49.

With A. M. WEIL. Le développement chez l'enfant de l'idée de patrie et des relations avec l'étranger. *Bulletin International des Sciences sociales.* Paris: UNESCO, 3, 605–621.

Du rapport des Sciences avec la Philosophie. *Synthèse,* 130–150.

Preface to R. Wavre: *La figure du monde: Essai sur le problème de l'espace, des Grecs à nos jours.* Neuchâtel: La Baconnière. Pp. 7–11.

1952

Essai sur les transformations des opérations logiques. Les 256 opérations ternaires de la logique bivalente des propositions. Paris: P. U. F.

Autobiographie. In C. Murchison & E. G. Boring (Eds.), *A History of Psychology in Autobiography.* Vol. 4. Worcester, Mass.: Clark University Press. Pp. 237–256.

De la psychologie génétique à l'épistémologie, *Diogène,* 1, 38–54.

La logistique axiomatique ou "pure," la logistique opératoire ou psychologique et les réalités auxquelles elles correspondent. *Methodos* (Milan), 72–84.

Quelques illusions géométriques renversées. *Revue suisse de Psychologie,* 11, 19–25.

Équilibre et structures d'ensemble (leçon inaugurale en Sorbonne). *Bulletin de Psychologie,* 1952/53, 6, numéro spécial, 4–10.

Contribution à la théorie générale des structures (I: intellectuelles; II: perceptives). *Proceedings and Papers of the XIIIth International Congress of Psychology at Stockholm, 1951.* Stockholm. Pp. 197–199.

1953

Logic and Psychology. Manchester: University Press, 1953. (Italian translation in preparation.)

Preface to R. Girod: *Attitudes collectives et relations humaines. Tendances actuelles des Sciences sociales américaines.* Paris: P. U. F. Pp. VII–IX.

With P. Osterrieth. L'évolution de l'illusion d'Oppel-Kundt en fonction de l'âge. *Archives de Psychologie,* 34, 1–38.

With M. Lambercier. La comparaison des différences de hauteur dans de plan fronto-parallèle. *Archives de Psychologie,* 34, 73–107.

With M. Denis-Prinzhorn. L'estimation perceptive des côtés du rectangle. *Archives de Psychologie,* 34, 109–131.

La période des opérations formelles et le passage de la logique de l'enfant à celle de l'adolescent. *Bulletin de Psychologie,* 1953/54, 7, 247–253.

How Children Form Mathematical Concepts. *Scientific American,* 189 (5), 74–79.

Structures opérationnelles et cybernétiques. *Actes de la 1re* Session d'études de l'Association de Psychologie scientifique de langue française: Le système nerveux et la psychologie, Paris, 1952. *Année psychologique*, 53(1), 379–388.

La centration perceptive et les illusions primaires et secondaires. Actes de la Société française de Psychologie (séance du 7 mars 1953). *L'année psychologique*, 53, 722–724.

Méthode axiomatique et méthode opérationnelle. *Synthèse*, 23–43.

1954

La vie et la pensée, du point de vue de la psychologie expérimentale et de l'épistémologie génétique. *VIIe Congrès des Sociétés de Philosophie de langue française, Grenoble, 1954,* 17–23.

Le langage et la pensée du point de vue génétique. In G. Revesz (Ed.), *Thinking and Speaking.* (Symposium.) Amsterdam: North Holland. Pp. 51–60.

Problems of Consciousness in Child Psychology: Developmental Changes in Awareness. (Trans. by E. Meyer.) In H. A. Abramson (Ed.), *Problems in Consciousness. Transactions of the IVth Conference, 1953, Princeton, N.J.* New York: J. Macy Foundation. Pp. 136–177.

With F. MAIRE & F. PRIVAT. La résistance des bonnes formes à l'illusion de Müller-Lyer. *Archives de Psychologie*, 34, 155–202.

With B. STETTLER VON ALBERTINI. Observation sur la perception des bonnes formes chez l'enfant par actualisation des lignes virtuelles. *Archives de Psychologie*, 34, 203–242.

With A. MORF. L'action des facteurs spatiaux et temporels de centration dans l'estimation visuelle des longueurs. *Archives de Psychologie*, 34, 243–288.

With M. DENIS-PRINZHORN. L'illusion des quadrilatères partiellement superposés chez l'enfant et chez l'adulte. *Archives de Psychologie*, 34, 289–321.

Ce qui subsiste de la théorie de la Gestalt dans la Psychologie contemporaine de l'intelligence et de la perception. *Revue suisse de Psychologie*, 13, 72–83.

Inconditionnés transcendantaux et épistémologie génétique. *Dialectica*, 8, 5–13.

Les relations entre l'affectivité et l'intelligence dans le développement mental de l'enfant. Paris: C. D. U.

1955

With B. INHELDER. *De la logique de l'enfant à la logique de l'adolescent.* Paris: P. U. F.

Translation:

The Growth of Logical Thinking from Childhood to Adolescence. (An essay on the construction of formal operational structures.) (Trans. by A. Parsons & S. Seagrim.) New York: Basic Books, 1958.

Preface to W. D. Wall: *Éducation et santé mentale.* Paris: UNESCO, 1955. Pp. 5–6.

Les lignes générales de l'épistémologie génétique. *Actes du IIe Congrès de l'Union Internationale de Philosophie des Sciences. Zurich, 1954.* Neuchâtel: Édition du Griffon. Pp. 26–45.

The Development of Time Concepts in the Child. In P. H. Hoch & J. Zubin (Eds.), *Psychology of Childhood.* New York: Grune and Stratton. Pp. 34–44.

Perceptual and Cognitive (or Operational) Structures in the Development of the Concept of Space in the Child. *Proceedings and Papers of the XIVth International Congress of Psychology, Montreal 1954.* Amsterdam: North Holland. Pp. 41–46.

Les structures mathématiques et les structures opératoires de l'intelligence. In J. Piaget *et al.* (Eds.), *L'enseignement des mathématiques.* Neuchâtel & Paris: Delachaux & Niestlé. Pp. 11–34. (Reedition 1965.)

Translation:

La enseñanza de las matemáticas. (Trans. by A. Maillo.) Madrid: Aguilar.

Essai d'une nouvelle interprétation probabiliste des effets de centration de la loi de Weber et de celle des centrations relatives. *Archives de Psychologie,* 35, 1–24.

With A. MORF. Note sur l'illusion des droites inclinées. *Archives de Psychologie,* 35, 65–76.

With F. PÈNE. Essai sur l'illusion de la médiane des angles en tant que mesure de l'illusion des angles. *Archives de Psychologie,* 35, 77–92.

La perception. *Rapport au IIe Symposium de l'Association de Psychologie scientifique de langue française, Louvain, 1953.* Paris: P. U. F. Pp. 17–30. Discussion: pp. 49–51, 52, 59–60, 78–81.

1956

Preface to L. Muller: *Recherches sur la compréhension des règles algébriques chez l'enfant.* Neuchâtel & Paris: Delachaux & Niestlé. Pp. 1–3.

Centration et décentration perceptives et représentatives. *Rivista di Psicologia,* Firenze, 50(4).

Motricité, perception et intelligence. *Enfance,* 9(2), 9–14.

With VINH BANG. Comparaison de l'illusion d'Oppel-Kundt au tachistoscope et en vision libre. Compte rendu des séances de la Société de Physique et d'Histoire naturelle de Genève. *Archives des Sciences physiques et naturelles,* 161, 210–213.

Problemy genetîcheskoi psikhologii. *Voprossy Psikhologuii,* Moskwa, 2, 30–47.

With E. VURPILLOT. La surestimation de la courbure des arcs de cercle. *Archives de Psychologie,* 35, 215–232.

With A. MORF. Note sur la comparaison des lignes perpendiculaires égales. *Archives de Psychologie,* 35, 233–255.

With M. LAMBERCIER. Grandeurs projectives et grandeurs réelles avec etalon éloigné. *Archives de Psychologie,* 35, 257–280.

With A. MORF. Les comparaisons verticales à faible intervalle. *Archives de Psychologie,* 35, 289–319.

With M. LAMBERCIER. Les comparaisons verticales à intervalles croissants. *Archives de Psychologie,* 35, 321–367.

Quelques impressions d'une visite aux psychologues soviétiques. *Bulletin international des Sciences sociales,* 8, 401–404.

Some Impressions of a Visit to Soviet Psychologists. *American Psychologist,* 11, 343–345.

Some Impressions of a Visit to Soviet Psychologists. *Acta Psychologica,* 12, 216–219.

In J. M. Tanner & B. Inhelder (Eds.), *Discussions on Child Development. The Proceedings of the First Meeting of the World Health Organization Study Group on the Psychobiological Development of the Child. Geneva 1953.* London: Tavistock Publications. Vol. 1. Biography: pp. 31–33; Discussion: pp. 31–33, 69–70, 71, 89–90, 93–94, 101, 104–105, 149.

Translation:

In J. M. Tanner & B. Inhelder (Eds.), *Entretiens sur le développement psycho-biologique de l'enfant.* (Trans. by D. Jullien-Vollmer.) Neuchâtel & Paris: Delachaux &

Niestlé, 1960. Biography: pp. 32–34; Discussion: pp. 74–75, 76–77, 96–97, 100, 108–109, 112–113, 161.

In J. M. Tanner & B. Inhelder (Eds.), *Discussions on Child Development. The Proceedings of the Second Meeting of the World Health Organization Study Group on the Psychobiological Development of the Child. London, 1954.* London: Tavistock Publications. Vol. 2. Discussion: pp. 24, 58–60, 61, 62.

Les stades du développement intellectuel de l'enfant et de l'adolescent. *Le Problème des Stades en Psychologie de l'Enfant. IIIe Symposium de l'Association de Psychologie scientifique de langue française. Genève, 1955.* Paris: P. U. F. Pp. 33–42; Discussion: pp. 56–61, 73–74.

Translation:

> *Los estadios en la psicologia del niño.* Buenos Aires: Editorial Lautario, 1963. Pp. 40–49; Discussion: pp. 82–116.

1957

Études d'épistémologie génétique I:

Le Centre international d'Épistémologie génétique et les Études d'Épistémologie génétique. Introduction to Vol. I. *Épistémologie génétique et recherche psychologique,* by E. W. BETH, W. MAYS, & J. PIAGET. Paris: P. U. F. Pp. 1–13.

Programme et méthodes de l'Épistémologie génétique. *Ibid.,* pp. 13–84.

Translation:

> *Epistemologia genetica e investigacion psicologica.* (Trans. by N. Bastard.) Buenos Aires: Nueva Vision, 1959.

Études d'épistémologie génétique II:

Logique et équilibre dans les comportements du sujet. In Vol. II: *Logique et équilibre,* by L. APOSTEL, B. MANDELBROT, & J. PIAGET. Paris: P. U. F. Pp. 27–117.

Études d'épistémologie génétique III:

Introduction to Vol. III: *Logique, langage et théorie de l'information,* by L. APOSTEL, B. MANDELBROT, & A. MORF. Paris: P. U. F. Pp. V–VI.

Études d'épistémologie génétique IV:

Les liaisons analytiques et synthétiques dans les comportements du sujet, by L. APOSTEL, W. MAYS, A. MORF, & J. PIAGET, with B. MATALON. Paris: P. U. F. Vol. IV.

L'actualité de J. A. Comenius. Preface to: *J. A. Comenius. Pages choisies.* Hommage de l'UNESCO à l'occasion du trois-centième anniversaire de la publication des "Opera didactica omnia," 1657–1957. Paris: UNESCO. Pp. 11–38.

Les activités mentales en rapport avec les expressions symboliques, logiques et mathématiques. *Synthèse,* 127–195.

Les notions de vitesse, d'espace parcouru et de temps chez l'enfant de 5 ans. *Enfance,* 10, 9–42.

The Child and Modern Physics. *Scientific American,* 196 (3), 46–51.

In, Colloque sur L'importance du mouvement dans le développement psychologique de l'enfant. *Psychologie française,* 2(1), 26–27.

Le mythe de l'origine sensorielle des connaissances scientifiques. *Actes de la Société helvétique des Sciences Naturelles,* 20–34.

Épistémologie de la relation. In, Anthony et al., *L'évolution humaine. Spéciation et relation.* Paris: Flammarion. Pp. 145–176.

1958

Études d'épistémologie génétique V:

La deuxième année d'activité et le deuxième Symposium du Centre International d'Épistémologie génétique. Introduction to Vol. V: *La lecture de l'expérience,* by A. JONCK-HEERE, B. MANDELBROT, & J. PIAGET. Paris: P. U. F. Pp. 1–27.

Assimilation et connaissance. *Ibid.,* pp. 49–108.

Études d'épistémologie génétique VI:

With A. MORF. Les isomorphismes partiels entre les structures logiques et les structures perceptives. In Vol. VI, *Logique et perception,* by J. S. BRUNER, F. BRESSON, A. MORF, & J. PIAGET. Paris: P. U. F. Pp. 49–116.

With A. MORF. Les préinférences perceptives et leurs relations avec les schèmes sensori-moteurs et opératoires. *Ibid.,* pp. 117–155.

With M. LAMBERCIER. La causalité perceptive visuelle chez l'enfant et chez l'adulte. *Archives de Psychologie,* 36, 77–201.

With J. MAROUN. La localisation des impressions d'impact dans la causalité perceptive tactilo-kinesthésique. *Archives de Psychologie,* 36, 202–235.

With M. WEINER. Quelques interférences entre la perception de la vitesse et la causalité perceptive. *Archives de Psychologie*, 36, 236–252.

With Y. FELLER & E. McNEAR. Essai sur la perception des vitesses chez l'enfant et chez l'adulte. *Archives de Psychologie*, 36, 253–327.

With VINH BANG & B. MATALON. Note on the Law of the Temporal Maximum of Some Opticogeometric Illusions. *The American Journal of Psychology*, 71 (Dallenbach commemorative number), 277–282.

In J. M. Tanner & B. Inhelder (Eds.), *Discussions on Child Development*. The Proceedings of the Third Meeting of the World Health Organization Study Group on the Psychobiological Development of the Child. Geneva, 1955. London: Tavistock Publications. Vol. 3. Discussion: pp. 114, 154–156, 157.

In, *Le conditionnement et l'apprentissage. IVe Symposium de l'Association de Psychologie scientifique de langue française.* Strasbourg 1956. Paris: P. U. F. Discussion: pp. 158–165.

1959

With B. INHELDER. *La genèse des structures logiques élémentaires, classifications et sériations.* Neuchâtel & Paris: Delachaux & Niestlé.

Translations:

The Early Growth of Logic in the Child (Classification and Seriation). (Trans. by G. A. Lunzer & D. Papert.) London: Routledge and Kegan Paul, 1964. New York: Harper, 1964.

Genezis elementarnih logičeskih struktur. (Trans. by E. M. Pcelkina.) Moskwa Izd. inostr. Lit., 1963.

Études d'épistémologie génétique VII:

La troisième année d'activité du Centre et le troisième Symposium international d'Épistémologie génétique. Introduction to Vol. VII: *Apprentissage et connaissance*, by P. GRÉCO & J. PIAGET. Paris: P. U. F. Pp. 1–20.

Apprentissage et connaissance (première partie). *Ibid.*, pp. 21–67.

Études d'épistémologie génétique X.

Apprentissage et connaissance (seconde partie). In, Vol. X: *La logique des apprentissages*, by M. GOUSTARD, P. GRÉCO, B. MATALON, & J. PIAGET. Paris: P. U. F. Pp. 159–188.

L'Institut des Sciences de l'Éducation de 1914 à 1956. *L'Histoire de l'Université de Genève.* Geneva: Georg, 4, 307–316.

Les modèles abstraits sont-ils opposés aux interprétations psychophysiologiques dans l'explication en psychologie? Esquisse et autobiographie intellectuelle. (Avec une photographie et un manuscrit fac-similé.) *Bulletin de Psychologie,* 1959–60, 13(1–2), No. 169, 7–13.

With J. RUTSCHMANN & B. MATALON. Nouvelles mesures des effets de centration en présentation tachistoscopique. *Archives de Psychologie,* 37, 140–165.

Perception, apprentissage et empirisme. *Dialectica,* 13, 5–15.

Le rôle de la notion d'équilibre dans l'explication en psychologie. Actes du XVe Congrès International de Psychologie, Bruxelles 1957. *Acta Psychologica,* 15, 51–52.

Pourquoi la formation des notions ne s'explique jamais par la seule perception. *Acta Psychologica,* 15, 314–316.

Die relationale Methode in der Psychologie der Wahrnehmung. (Trans. by K. Witte.) *Zeitschrift für experimentelle und angewandte Psychologie,* 6, 78–94.

1960

Études d'épistémologie génétique XI:

La quatrième année d'activité (1958–59) et le quatrième Symposium (22–26 juin 1959) du Centre International d'Épistémologie génétique. Problèmes de la construction du nombre. Introduction to Vol. XI: *Problèmes de la construction du nombre,* by P. GRÉCO, J. B. GRIZE, S. PAPERT, & J. PIAGET. Paris: P. U. F. Pp. 1–68.

Études d'épistémologie génétique XII:

La portée psychologique et épistémologique des essais néohulliens de D. Berlyne. In, Vol. XII: *Théorie du comportement et opérations,* by D. E. BERLYNE & J. PIAGET. Paris: P. U. F. Pp. 105–123.

Chronique de l'Institut des Sciences de l'Éducation, Section Psychologie. *Bastions de Genève,* No. 5, 102–105.

Genèse actuelle et maxima perceptifs. *Proceedings of the Sixteenth International Congress of Psychology. Bonn, 1960.* Amsterdam: North Holland. Pp. 81–82.

Développement et apprentissage perceptif. *Ibid.,* pp. 323–325.

Preface to M. Margot: *L'École opérante. Psychopédagogie de l'élaboration mathématique.* Neuchâtel & Paris: Delachaux & Niestlé. Pp. I–II.

Les praxies chez l'enfant. *Revue neurologique,* 102(6), 551–565.

L'aspect génétique de l'œuvre de Pierre Janet. *Psychologie française,* 5(2), 111–117.

Les modèles abstraits sont-ils opposés aux interprétations psychophysiologiques dans l'explication en psychologie? *Revue suisse de Psychologie,* 14, 57–65.

Problèmes de la psycho-sociologie de l'enfance. In Gurvitch (Ed.), *Traité de Sociologie.* Paris: P. U. F. Vol. 2. Pp. 229–254.

Wahrnehmungskonstanzen und Kausalitätswahrnehmung. *Psychologische Beitrage,* 1–2, 183–229.

In J. M. Tanner & B. Inhelder (Eds.), *Discussions on Child Development.* The Proceedings of the Fourth Meeting of the World Health Organization Study Group on the Psychobiological Development of the Child. Geneva, 1956. London: Tavistock Publications. Vol. 4: The general problems of the psychological development of the child, pp. 3–27. Discussions: pp. 77–83, 89–94, 95–96, 98–105, 106, 108–109, 110–111, 116–119, 120–121, 121–123, 124, 126, 130, 132, 171–172, 173–174.

Individual and Collective Problems in the Study of Thinking. *Annals of the New York Academy of Sciences,* 91, 22–37.

1961

Les mécanismes perceptifs. Modèles probabilistes, analyse génétique, relations avec l'intelligence. Paris: P. U. F.

Études d'épistémologie génétique XIV:
 Épistémologie mathématique et psychologie, by E. W. BETH & J. PIAGET. Paris: P. U. F. Vol. XIV: 2nd part, pp. 143–324; with E. W. Beth: general conclusions pp. 325–332.

Rapports sur les travaux de psychologie de l'enfant effectués dans les écoles de Genève en 1960–1961. Geneva: I. S. E.

The Language and Thought of the Child. In, *Classics in Psychology.* New York: Thorno Shipley. Pp. 994–1031.

Defense de l'Épistémologie génétique. *Revue philosophique,* 475–500. (Reproduit in *Ét. Épist. Génét.,* xvi, v. à 1962.)

The Genetic Approach to the Psychology of Thought. *Journal of Educational Psychology,* 52(6), 275–281.

With VINH BANG. L'évolution de l'illusion des espaces divisés (Oppel-Kundt) en présentation tachistoscopique. *Archives de Psychologie,* 38, 1–21.

With B. Matalon & Vinh Bang. L'évolution de l'illusion dite "verticale-horizontale," de ses composantes (rectangle et équerre) et de l'illusion de Delbœuf en présentation tachistoscopique. *Archives de Psychologie*, 23–68.

With A. Morf. La comparaison des verticales et des horizontales dans la figure en équerre. *Archives de Psychologie*, 69–88.

With Vinh Bang. L'enregistrement des mouvements oculaires en jeu chez l'adulte dans la comparaison verticales, horizontales et obliques et dans les perceptions de la figure en équerre. *Archives de Psychologie*, 89–141.

With Vinh Bang. Comparaison des mouvements oculaires et des centrations du regard chez l'enfant et chez l'adulte. *Archives de Psychologie*, 167–199.

1962
Études d'épistémologie génétique XVI:
Introduction to Vol. XVI: *Implication, formalisation et logique naturelle*, by E. W. Beth, J. B. Grize, R. Martin, B. Matalon, A. Naess, & J. Piaget. Paris: P. U. F. Pp. 1–7.

Défense dé l'Épistémologie génétique. *Ibid.*, pp. 165–191.

Preface to T. Gouin-Décarie: *Intelligence et affectivité chez le jeune enfant*. Neuchâtel & Paris: Delachaux & Niestlé. Pp. 5–8.

Preface to M. Laurendeau & A. Pinard: *La pensée causale. Étude génétique et expérimentale*. Paris: P. U. F. Pp. 7–11.

With B. Inhelder. Le développement des images mentales chez l'enfant. *Journal de psychologie normale et pathologique*, 59(1–2), 75–108.

Le rôle de l'imitation dans la formation de la représentation. *Évolution psychiatrique* (en hommage à H. Wallon), 27(1), 141–150.

With Y. Feller & M. Bovet. La perception de la durée en fonction des vitesses. *Archives de Psychologie*, 38, 1–55.

Le temps et le développement intellectuel de l'enfant. *La vie et le temps. Rencontres internationales de Genève, 1962. Collection Histoire et Société d'aujourd'hui*. Neuchâtel: La Baconnière. Pp. 35–38. Discussions: Le temps du développement psychologique, pp. 179–192; Sciences normatives et éducation, pp. 201–209.

Comments on Vygotsky's Critical Remarks Concerning the Language and Thought of the Child, and Judgment and Reasoning in the Child. (No. 8.) Cambridge, Mass.: M.I.T. Press. Three Lectures: The Stages of the Intellectual Development of the Child; The Relation of Affectivity to Intelligence in the Mental Development of the Child; Will and Action. *Bulletin of the Menninger Clinic* (Topeka, Kansas), 26(3), 120–145.

1963
Études d'épistémologie génétique XV:
  Le problème de la filiation des structures. Introduction to Vol. XV: *La filiation des structures,* by L. APOSTEL, J. B. GRIZE, S. PAPERT, & J. PIAGET. Paris: P. U. F. Pp. 1–23.
Études d'épistémologie génétique XVII:
  Les travaux de l'année 1959–1960 et le Ve Symposium du Centre international d'Épistémologie génétique. In, Vol. XVII: *La formation des raisonnements récurrentiels,* by P. GRÉCO, B. INHELDER, B. MATALON, & J. PIAGET. Paris: P. U. F. Pp. 3–46.
With B. INHELDER. De l'itération des actions à la récurrence élémentaire. *Ibid.,* pp. 47–120.
Preface to M. Nassefat: *Étude quantitative sur l'évolution des opérations intellectuelles.* Neuchâtel & Paris: Delachaux & Niestlé.
Preface to E. Vurpillot: *L'organisation perceptive, son rôle dans l'évolution des illusions optico-géométriques.* Paris: Vrin. Pp. 7–8.
L'explication en psychologie et le parallélisme psychophysiologique. *Traité de Psychologie expérimentale* (Paul Fraisse et Jean Piaget Eds.), tome I: *Histoire et Méthode.* Paris: P. U. F. Pp. 121–152.
Le développement des perceptions en fonction de l'âge. *Ibid.,* tome VI: *La perception.* Paris: P. U. F. Pp. 1–57.
With B. INHELDER. Les images mentales. *Ibid.,* tome VII: *L'Intelligence.* Paris: P. U. F. Pp. 65–108.
With B. INHELDER. Les opérations intellectuelles et leur développement. *Ibid.,* pp. 109–155.
With S. PAPERT. Note sur les relations entre les illusions de Müller-Lyer et de Delbœuf. *Année psychologique,* 63, 351–357.

Problèmes psychologiques et épistémologiques du temps. *Cahiers de psychologie* (Société de Psychologie du Sud-Est), 6(4), 217–237.

Le langage et les opérations intellectuelles. In, *Problèmes de psycholinguistique. Symposium de l'Association de psychologie scientifique de langue française, Neuchâtel, 1962.* Paris: P. U. F. Pp. 51–61. Discussion: pp. 71–72.

1964

Six études de psychologie. Geneva: Éd. Gonthier.

1. Le développement mental de l'enfant. Zurich, *Juventus Helvetica,* 1943.
2. La pensée du jeune enfant. Conférence prononcée à l'Institute of Education, Université de Londres, 1963.
3. Le langage et la pensée du point de vue génétique. *Acta Psychologica,* Amsterdam, 1954, Vol. 10.
4. Le rôle de la notion d'équilibre dans l'explication en psychologie. *Acta Psychologica,* Amsterdam, 1959, Vol. 15.
5. Problèmes de psychologie génétique. *Voprossi Psykhologuii,* Moscou, 1956.
6. Entretiens sur les notions de "genèse" et de "structure." *Congrès et Colloques,* Vol. 8. La Haye-Paris: Mouton & Cie, 1964.

Études d'épistémologie génétique XVIII:

Les travaux de l'année 1960–1961 et le VIᵉ Symposium (19–24 juin 1961) du Centre international d'Épistémologie génétique. Introduction to Vol. XVIII: *L'épistémologie de l'espace,* by V. Bang, P. Gréco, J. B. Grize, Y. Hatwell, J. Piaget, G. N. Seagrim, & E. Vurpillot. Paris: P. U. F. Pp. 1–40.

Classification des disciplines et connexions interdisciplinaires. *Revue internationale des Sciences sociales,* 16, 598–616.

Cognitive Development in Children (Development and Learning; The Development of Mental Imagery; Mother Structures and the Notion of Number; Relations Between the Notions of Time and Speed in Children). In R. Ripple & V. Rockcastle (Eds.), *Piaget Rediscovered. Report of the Conference on Cognitive Studies and Curriculum Development. Cornell University.* Pp. 6–48.

Genèse et structure en psychologie de l'intelligence. In *Entretiens sur les notions de "genèse" et de "structure."* Congrès et colloques, Vol. 8. La Haye-Paris: Mouton & Cie.

1965

Sagesse et illusion de la philosophie. Paris: P. U. F.

Études sociologiques. Geneva: Droz.
1. Explication en sociologie. In, *Introduction à l'épistémologie génétique,* tome III: *La pensée biologique, la pensée psychologique et la pensée sociologique.* Paris: P. U. F., 1951.
2. Essai sur la théorie des valeurs qualitatives en sociologie statique ("synchronique"). In, *Publications de la Faculté des Sciences économiques et sociales de l'Université de Genève.* Geneva: Georg, 1941.
3. Les opérations logiques et la vie sociale. *Ibid.,* 1945.
4. Les relations entre la morale et le droit. *Ibid.,* 1944.

With B. INHELDER. *Rapport sur les travaux de psychologie de l'enfant effectués dans les écoles de Genève.* Geneva: I. S. E.

Preface to B. Beauverd: *Avant le calcul. Cahiers de pédagogie expérimentale et de psychologie de l'enfant.* Neuchâtel & Paris: Delachaux & Niestlé, 21, 1–2.

Langage et pensée. *La Revue du Praticien,* tome XV, 17, 2253–2254.

Éducation et instruction depuis 1955. *Encyclopédie Française.* Mise à jour du tome 15: *Éducation et Instruction,* 7–45.

Psychology and Philosophy. (Trans. by R. Howard.) In Wohlman & Nagel (Eds.), *Scientific Psychology, Principles and Approach.* New York & London: Basic Books. Pp. 28–43.

1966

With B. INHELDER. *La psychologie de l'enfant.* Collection "Que sais-je." Paris: P. U. F.

With B. INHELDER. *L'image mentale chez l'enfant. Étude sur le développement des représentations imagées* (avec la collaboration de M. Bovet, A. Etienne, F. Frank, E. Schmid, S. Taponier et T. Vinh Bang). Paris: P. U. F.

Time Perception in Children. (Trans. by B. Montgomery.) In J. P. Frazer (Ed.), *The Voices of Time.* New York: G. Braziller. Pp. 202–216.

Response to Brian Sutton-Smith. *Psychological Review,* 73, 111–112.

Études d'épistémologie génétique XX:
Les travaux des années 1961–1963 et les Symposiums VII et VIII (juin 1962 et juin 1963) du Centre international

d'Épistémologie génétique. Problèmes du temps et de la fonction. Chap. 1 of Vol. XX: *L'Épistémologie du Temps*, by J. B. Grize, K. Henry, M. Meylan-Backs, F. Orsini, J. Piaget, & N. Van den Bogaert. Paris: P. U. F. Pp. 1–66. With the collaboration of Marianne Meylan-Backs. Comparaisons et opérations temporelles en relation avec la vitesse et la fréquence. *Ibid.*, pp. 67–106.

Nécessité et signification des recherches comparatives en psychologie génétique. *Journal international de Psychologie*, 1, 3–13.

Foreword to Millie Almy, with Edward Chittenden and Paula Miller: *Young Children's Thinking, Studies of Some Aspects of Piaget's Theory*. New York: Teachers College Press, Columbia University.

1967

Logique et connaissance scientifique. In R. Queneau (Ed.), *Encyclopédie de la Pléïade*. Paris: Gallimard.

Biologie et connaissance. Coll. L'avenir de la science. Paris: Gallimard.

1968

With H. Sinclair-de Zwarts. *Mémoire et intelligence*. Paris: P. U. F.

Le Structuralisme. Paris: P. U. F.

Works and articles in press:

Henri Piéron, 1881–1964. *American Journal of Psychology*.

Logique formelle et psychologie génétique. In P. Fraisse, J. M. Faverge, & F. Bresson (Eds.), *Les modèles formels en Psychologie* (publication du CNRS). Paris.

Works and articles in preparation:

Intelligence et adaptation biologique. *Symposium de l'Association de Psychologie scientifique et langue française, Marseille, 1965.*

Problèmes généraux dans les recherches interdisciplinaires et mécanismes communs. UNESCO.

Tendances actuelles de la psychologie et ses relations avec les autres sciences. UNESCO.

Observations sur le mode d'insertion et la chute des rameaux secondaires chez les Sedum. Essai sur un cas d'anticipation morphogénétique interprété causalement. In *Candollea*.

Psychologie et philosophie. Débat de J. Piaget avec P. Fraisse, Y. Galifret, F. Jeanson, P. Ricoeur, R. Zazzo, à propos de *Sagene et illusions de la Philosophie*. Paris: Union Rationaliste.

Introduction to *L'homme à la découverte de lui-même*. Vol. 5 of *L'aventure humaine*. Geneva: Kister La conscience.

BIBLIOGRAPHY

Baldwin, A. L. *Behavior and Development in Childhood.* New York: Dryden Press, 1955.

———. *Theories of Child Development.* New York: John Wiley & Sons, 1968.

Bandura, A. and Walters, R. H. *Social Learning and Personality Development.* New York: Holt, Rinehart & Winston, Inc., 1963.

Beilin, H. "Stimulus and Cognitive Transformation in Conservation." In D. Elkind and J. H. Flavell (eds.), *Studies in Cognitive Development: Essays in Honor of Jean Piaget.* New York: Oxford University Press, 1969, pp. 409–437.

Berlyne, D. E. "Recent Developments in Piaget's Work." *British Journal of Educational Psychology,* 1957, 27: 1–12.

———. *Structure and Direction in Thinking.* New York: John Wiley & Sons, 1965.

Bowlby, J. *Attachment.* New York: Basic Books, Inc., 1969.

Brearley, Molly, and Elizabeth Hitchfield. *A Guide to Reading Piaget.* New York: Schocken Books, 1966.

Bruner, J. S., Goodnow, J. J., and Austin, G. A. *A Study of Thinking.* New York: Science Editions, 1952.

Bruner, J. S., Olver, R. R., and Greenfield, P. M. *Studies in Cognitive Growth.* New York: John Wiley & Sons, 1966.

Cannon, W. B. "Hunger and Thirst," *A Handbook of General Psychology* (C. Murchison, ed.). Worcester, Mass.: Clark University Press, 1934.

Chomsky, N. *Language and Mind.* New York: Harcourt, Brace and World, 1968.

Décarie, T. Gouin. *Intelligence and Affectivity in Early Childhood.* New York: International Universities Press, 1965.

Durkheim, E. *Sociology and Philosophy* (translated by D. F. Pocook). Glencoe, Ill.: Free Press, 1953.

Evans, R. I. *Conversations with Carl Jung and Reactions from Ernest Jones.* New York: D. Van Nostrand, Inc., 1964.

———. *Dialogue with Erich Fromm.* New York: Harper & Row, 1966.

———. *B. F. Skinner: The Man and His Ideas.* New York: E. P. Dutton & Co., Inc., 1968.

———. *Dialogue with Erik Erikson.* New York: E. P. Dutton & Co., Inc., 1969a.

———. *Psychology and Arthur Miller.* New York: E. P. Dutton & Co., Inc., 1969b.

———. "Contributions to the History of Psychology: X Filmed Dialogues with Notable Contributors to Psychology." *Psychological Reports,* 1969c, 25, 159–164.

———. *Gordon Allport: The Man and His Ideas.* New York: E. P. Dutton & Co., Inc., 1971.

Flavell, John H. *The Developmental Psychology of Jean Piaget.* Princeton: D. Van Nostrand Co., Inc., 1963.

Furth, H. G. *Piaget for Teachers.* Englewood Cliffs, New Jersey: Prentice-Hall, Inc., 1970.

Ginsburg, Herbert, and Sylvia Opper. *Piaget's Theory of Intellectual Development.* New Jersey: Prentice-Hall, Inc., 1969.

Hebb, D. O. *Organization of Behavior.* New York: John Wiley & Sons, 1949.

Hull, C. L. *Principles of Behavior.* New York: Appleton, 1943.

Jensen, A. "How Much Can We Boost IQ and Scholastic Achievement?" *Harvard Educational Review,* 1969, pp. 1–123.

Kessen, William, and Clement Kuhlman (eds.). "Thought in the Young Child," *Monograph of the Society for Research and Child Development.* 1962, 27: 2.

Maier, Henry. *Three Theories of Child Development.* New York: Harper & Row, 1965.

Mead, G. H. *Philosophy of the Present.* La Salle, Ill.: Open Court Publishing, 1932.

Montessori, M. *The Montessori Method* (translated by A. E. George). New York: Schocken Books, 1964.

Nash, J. *Developmental Psychology: A Psychobiological Approach.* New Jersey: Prentice-Hall, Inc., 1970.

Phillips, John L., Jr. *The Origins of Intellect: Piaget's Theory.* San Francisco: W. H. Freeman & Company, 1969.

Piaget, Jean. *Play, Dreams and Imitation.* New York: W. H. Norton & Co., Inc., 1951.

———. *Psychology of Intelligence.* New Jersey: Littlefield, Adams & Co., 1960.

———. *Six Psychological Studies.* New York: Vintage Books, 1968.

————. *The Child's Conception of Physical Causality.* Totowa: Littlefield, Adams, & Co., 1969.

————. *The Language and Thought of the Child.* London: Routledge & Kegan Paul Ltd., 1950.

Rosenthal, R. *Experimenter Effects in Behavioral Research.* New York: Appleton-Century-Crofts, 1966.

Rousseau, J. J. *Émile* (translated by B. Foxley). New York: E. P. Dutton & Co., Inc., 1925.

Skinner, B. F. *Verbal Behavior.* New York: Appleton-Century-Crofts, 1968.

Spitz, R. A. *The First Year of Life.* New York: International Universities Press, 1965.

Thorndike, E. L. "Animal Intelligence. An Experimental Study of the Associative Processes in Animals." *Psychological Monographs,* 1898, 2, No. 8.

Tolman, E. C. *Purposive Behavior in Animals and Men.* New York: Century, 1932.

Tuddenham, Read D. "Jean Piaget and the World of the Child." *American Psychology.* 1966, 21: 207–17.

INDEX

ABOUT THE AUTHOR

RICHARD I. EVANS received his Ph.D. from Michigan State University and is currently professor of psychology at the University of Houston. He is the Director of the Social Psychology/Behavioral Medicine Research and Graduate Training Group.

A National Science Foundation grant has enabled him to film discussions and complete books with some of the world's foremost behavioral scientists including the distinguished participants in the dialogues in this Praeger Series.

He is a pioneer in public television and in the social psychology of communication, and has published over a hundred articles in the area of social psychology. In addition to the volumes in this Dialogue Series, his books include *Social Psychology in Life* (with Richard Rozelle), *Resistance in Innovation in Higher Education, The Making of Psychology,* and *The Making of Social Psychology.*

His recent honors include the American Psychological Foundation Media Awards for the book, *Gordon Allport: The Man and His Ideas* and the film, "A Psychology of Creativity." He and his colleagues received American Psychological Association Division 13 Research Excellence Awards in 1970, 1973, and 1977 for their work in social psychology in behavioral medicine. He received the Phi Kappa Phi National Distinguished Scholar Award for the 1974-77 Triennium, and the 1980 Ester Farfel Award, the University of Houston's highest award for excellence in teaching, research and service.

M